Mechanics, Grammar, & Usage
Grades 2-3

W9-ANG-350

Turn to each section to find a more detailed skills list.

Table of Contents

What Does This Book Include?

- More than 75 student practice pages that reinforce basic mechanics, grammar, and usage skills
- A detailed skills list for each section of the book
- Send-home letters that inform parents of the skills being targeted and ways to practice these skills
- Student checkups
- A reproducible student progress chart
- Awards to celebrate student progress
- Answer keys for easy checking
- Perforated pages for easy removal and filing if desired

What Are the Benefits of This Book?

- Organized for quick and easy use
- Enhances and supports your existing reading and writing programs
- Offers multiple practice opportunities
- Helps develop mastery of basic skills
- Provides reinforcement for different ability levels
- Includes communication pages that encourage parents' participation in their children's learning of reading and writing
- Contains checkups that assess students' mechanics, grammar, and usage knowledge
- Offers a reproducible chart for documenting student progress
- Aligns with national literacy standards

How to Use This Book
Steps to Success

Choose Skills to Target

Scan the detailed table of contents at the beginning of each section to find just the right skills to target your students' needs.

Select Fun Practice Pages

Choose from a variety of fun formats the pages that best match your students' current ability levels.

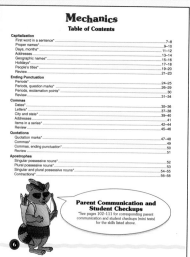

Fun Formats

Date Skill Completed

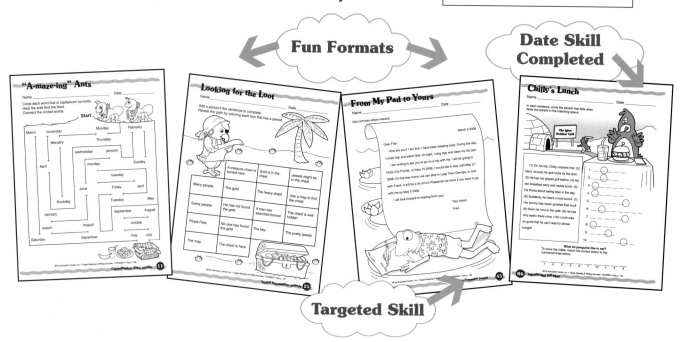

Targeted Skill

Letter to Parents Informing Them of Skill to Review

Communicate With Parents

Recruit parent assistance by locating the appropriate parent letter (pages 102–122), making copies, and sending the letter home.

Problems for Practice

Skills Review for Parents

Assess Student Understanding

Assess students' progress with student checkups (mini tests) on pages 103–123. Choose Checkup A or Checkup B.

Two Checkups for Each Skill

Document Progress

Documenting student progress can be as easy as 1, 2, 3! Do the following for each student:

1. Make a copy of the Student Progress Chart (page 101).
2. File the chart in his portfolio or a class notebook.
3. Record the date each checkup is given, the number of correct answers, and any comments regarding his progress.

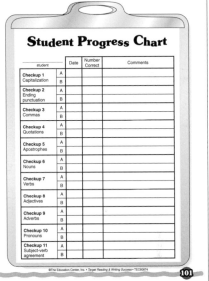

Student Progress Chart

student		Date	Number Correct	Comments
Checkup 1 Capitalization	A			
	B			
Checkup 2 Ending punctuation	A			
	B			
Checkup 3 Commas	A			
	B			
Checkup 4 Quotations	A			
	B			
Checkup 5 Apostrophes	A			
	B			
Checkup 6 Nouns	A			
	B			
Checkup 7 Verbs	A			
	B			
Checkup 8 Adjectives	A			
	B			
Checkup 9 Adverbs	A			
	B			
Checkup 10 Pronouns	A			
	B			
Checkup 11 Subject-verb agreement	A			
	B			

©The Education Center, Inc. • *Target Reading & Writing Success* • TEC60874

101

Celebrate!

Celebrate mechanics, grammar, and usage success using the awards on page 124.

Great aim!

_____ student
is right on target with
_____ skill
_____ teacher
_____ date

©The Education Center, Inc. • *Target Reading & Writing Success* • TEC60874

You hit the bull's-eye!

_____ student
hit the mark with
_____ skill
_____ teacher
_____ date

©The Education Center, Inc. • *Target Reading & Writing Success* • TEC60874

Also Available From Your Friends at *The Mailbox*®

www.themailbox.com

Mechanics

Mechanics

Table of Contents

Parent Communication and Student Checkups

*See pages 102–111 for corresponding parent communication and student checkups (mini tests) for the skills listed above.

Pet Store Shoppers

Name _____ Date _____

Draw a box around each letter that should be capitalized.
If the sentence is capitalized correctly, color the pawprint.

Dog Supplies

now is the time to buy dog supplies!

try our new puppy shampoo.

Our doggy beds are soft and warm!

stock up on Furry Friends dog food.

Your dog will love our tasty treats!

buy a rubber ball or a chewy bone.

Be sure to pick up a toy too!

is it time for a new dog-food dish?

We have leashes in all lengths.

do you need a new dog brush?

We have collars in every color.

Ahoy, Mates!

Name _____   Date _____

Circle each letter that should be capitalized.
Each time you circle a letter, color one of the ship's portholes.

welcome aboard the SS *Hippo!*

captain Potamus will steer the ship.

he loves to sail the seas. the captain

and his crew take care of the boat.

they clean the deck and raise the

sail. captain Potamus also has a

noisy pet. pete the parrot rides on

the captain's shoulder. the captain

calls out orders to his crew. then

Pete repeats them. maybe his name

should be "Re-Pete"!

Capitalization: first word in a sentence

The Family Tree

Name _Molly E. Birdsall_   Date _____

Color the acorn if the name is capitalized correctly.
Circle each letter that should be capitalized.

Fred
e.
Frolic

Martin
Scurry

Natasha
Nutley

Amanda
Sue
Oakley

Clayton
Acorn

Sammy
squirrel

trevor
P.
Treemont

Charlie
B.
Chatter

Brandi
lynn
branch

liz
nester

jackie
Scamper
jr.

Jennifer
Frisky

Psst!
There are
10 missing
capital letters.

A Team With Pride

Name _____ Date _____

Underline each player's name.
Circle each letter that should be capitalized.
Write the correct capital letter above each circled letter.

The Mane Town Lions are on the field. Their quarterback,

ron roar, throws the football. The ball sails past henry Hall.

Next, it flies right through Frank fur's paws.

Just before it hits the ground, Karl king

makes an amazing catch! matt manesly

tries to tackle him. Pete padfoot tries

to bring him down. But karl gets by

them both and scores! Les lee kicks

the extra point. Hooray for

teamwork!

"A-maze-ing" Ants

Name _____ Date _____

Circle each word that is capitalized correctly.
Help the ants find the food.
Connect the circled words.

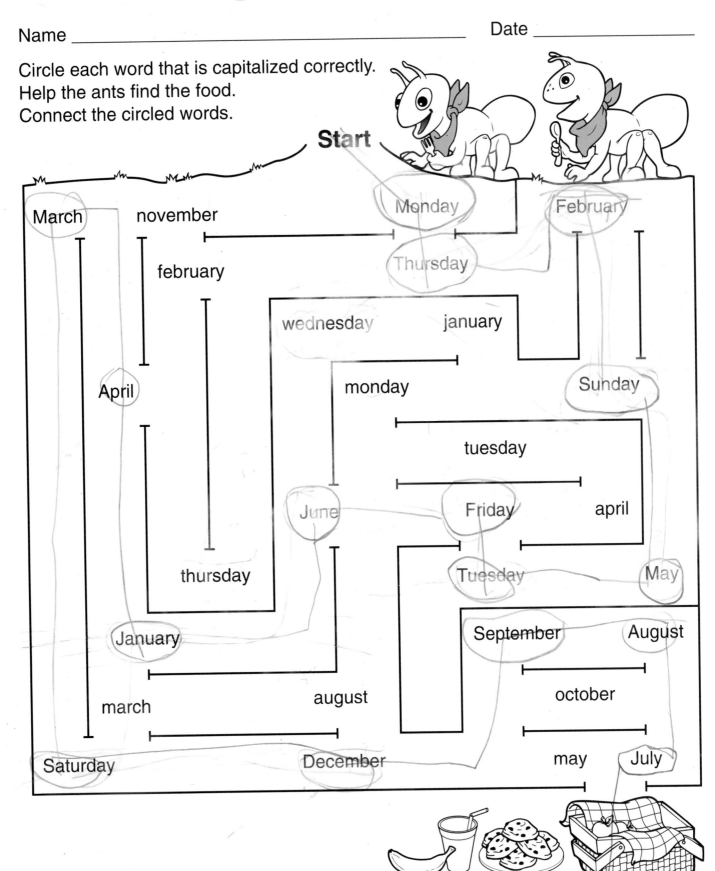

Start

March   november

february

Monday   February

Thursday

wednesday   january

monday   Sunday

April   tuesday

June   Friday   april

thursday   Tuesday   May

January   September   August

march   august   october

Saturday   December   may   July

A "Moo-velous" Treat

Name _____   Date _____

Circle each letter that should be capitalized.
Color one ice-cream scoop for each circled letter.
Write each date correctly.

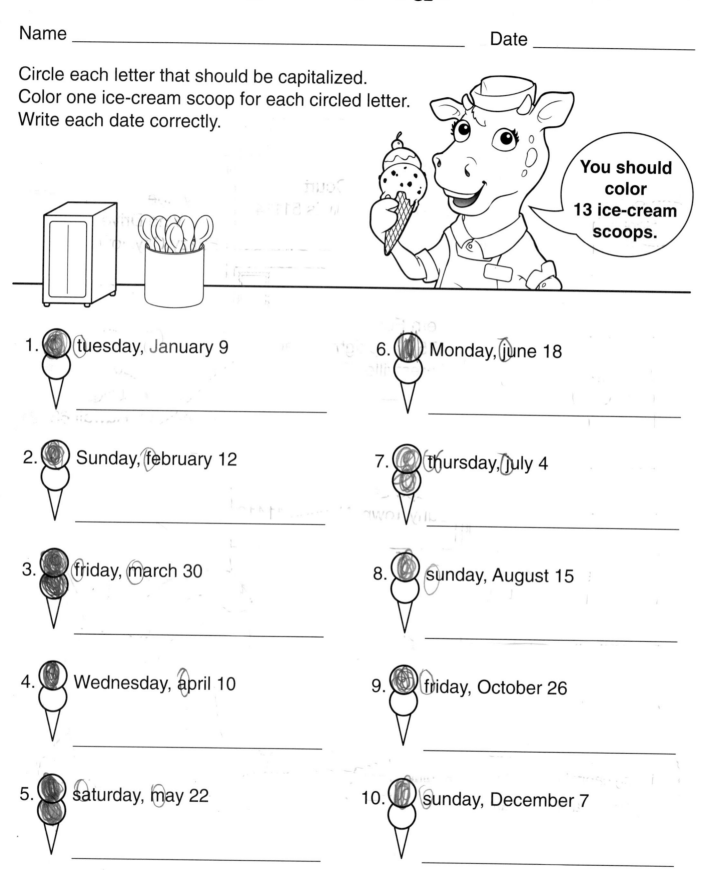

You should color 13 ice-cream scoops.

1. tuesday, January 9
_____

2. Sunday, february 12
_____

3. friday, march 30
_____

4. Wednesday, april 10
_____

5. saturday, may 22
_____

6. Monday, june 18
_____

7. thursday, july 4
_____

8. sunday, August 15
_____

9. friday, October 26
_____

10. sunday, December 7
_____

Monkeying Around

Name _____   Date _____

Circle each letter that should be capitalized.
Color each stamp by the code.

Bob Banana
54 Screeching Street
Chimptown, alaska 79635

Harry Foot
129 Treetop Court
jungle City, Illinois 51114

Amy Ape
514 Vine Drive
Fuzzy City, iowa 81765

Bo Baboon
63 Canopy Way
Tailboro, montana 36305

Fern Fur
475 Hang tight Terrace
Forestville, Florida 85419

Moe Monkey
23 Jungle street
Gorillaton, Hawaii 63121

Tony Tail
90 ape Lane
Curly Town, Nevada 11410

Glo Gorilla
18 High Tree Circle
Swinging vine, Ohio 44322

Color Code

missing capital in street name = blue

missing capital in city name = red

missing capital in state name = green

Lily Pad Leap

Name _____ Date _____

Circle each letter that should be capitalized.
Write the correct capital letter above each circled letter.

Each flower tells the number of errors on the lily pad.

3
268 lily Pad place
fresh Pond, Michigan

3
78 hopping road
Green lake, Arkansas

2
59 Toadstool Avenue
marshtown, maine

5
841 tadpole terrace
nut swamp, kansas

4
577 ribbit Road
bubbling brook, georgia

4
143 big leap court
frogport, Alabama

2
21 jumping Street
Streamdale, illinois

3
115 spotted road
croakville, Connecticut

Capitalization: addresses

Of Mice and Maps

Name _____   Date _____

Write each place name with the correct capitalization.

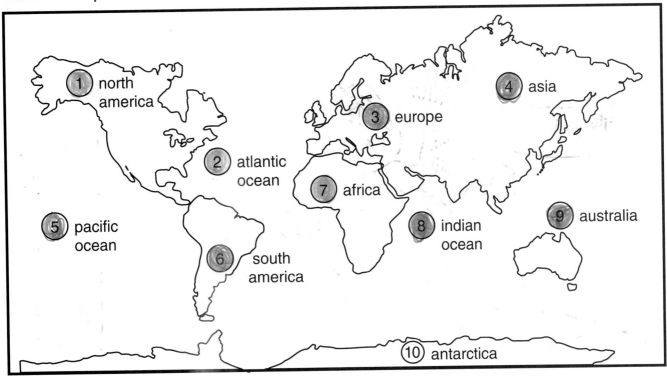

1. north america
2. atlantic ocean
3. europe
4. asia
5. pacific ocean
6. south america
7. africa
8. indian ocean
9. australia
10. antarctica

1. North America
2. Atlantic ocean
3. Europe
4. Asia
5. Pacific ocean
6. South america
7. Africa
8. Indian ocean
9. Australia
10. _____

A "Bear-y" Rugged Trip

Name _____ Date _____

Circle each letter that should be capitalized.

1. Bea and Barb Bear hike to mount grizzly.

2. Their hike begins at bat cave, in the middle of wild woods.

3. They row a boat across snake river.

4. When they reach sun valley, Barb takes a picture.

5. At heart's hill, the bears stop for lunch.

6. Then they hike through red rock range.

7. They stop to swim in snow lake.

8. At the end of wild woods, Barb takes another picture.

9. Then they see mount grizzly!

10. Next time, they will hike to mount flat top.

What do Bea and Barb wear in their hair?

To solve the riddle, color each letter you circled.
Write the remaining letters on the lines below.

B	B	W	W	E	M	M	M	A	R	R	R	R

R	W	W	F	E	H	H	V	T	T	T	E	C	L	G	G	S	S	S

" ___ ___ ___ ___ ___ ___ - ___ ___ ___ ___ ___ ___ ___ "

Capitalization: geographic names

A Quilt for All Seasons

Name _____ Date _____

Cross out each letter that should be capitalized.
Write the correct capital letter above each
   crossed-out letter.
For each holiday that is capitalized correctly,
   color the picture.

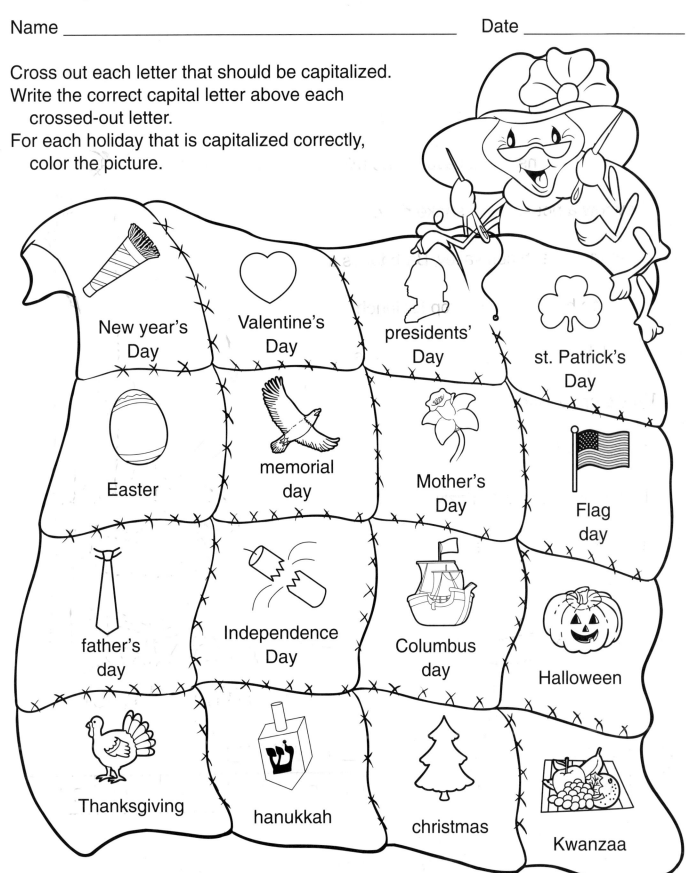

New year's Day

Valentine's Day

presidents' Day

st. Patrick's Day

Easter

memorial day

Mother's Day

Flag day

father's day

Independence Day

Columbus day

Halloween

Thanksgiving

hanukkah

christmas

Kwanzaa

Hog-Wild Holidays

Name _____ Date _____

Use a red crayon to draw a box around each holiday that is
   capitalized correctly.
Use a brown crayon to draw a box around each holiday
   that is not capitalized correctly.

Paul Pig loves holidays! The first holiday he celebrates each year is Martin luther king Jr. Day. On Valentine's Day, he gives paper hearts to his farm animal friends. He collects clovers for St. Patrick's day. Each easter, he thanks the chickens for their eggs. He is proud to display the flag on memorial Day, Flag Day, and the Fourth of July! In the fall, Paul dresses up for Halloween. Then he gets ready for Christmas, hanukkah, and kwanzaa. I guess you could say that Paul goes hog-wild for holidays!

©The Education Center, Inc. • *Target Reading & Writing Success* • TEC60874 • Key p. 127
Capitalization: holidays

All Abuzz!

Name _____ Date _____

If a person's title is capitalized correctly, color the flower yellow.
If a person's title is not capitalized correctly, rewrite it on the lines below.
Use the correct capitalization.

Dr.
Black

miss
Polly
Pollen

Captain
Will
Wasp

Mrs.
Honey
Comb

queen
Bumble

ms.
Y.
Jacket

mrs.
Cindy
Stripe

King
Buzz

Chief
Harvey
Hive

uncle
Hank
Hornet

Aunt
Busy
Bee

mr.
Dave
Drone

_____   _____

_____   _____

_____   _____

Capitalization: people's titles

Sharks in the Snow

Name _____   Date _____

Underline each person's title.
If a title is capitalized correctly, circle the letter
   in the yes column.
If a title is not capitalized correctly, circle the
   letter in the no column.

		Yes	No
1.	dr. Frank Finn lives at the north pole.	H	T
2.	He and Chief Tom Tooth are in a snowman-building contest.	R	S
3.	One of the judges is mr. Gus Gray.	?	!
4.	The other judge is queen Wanda White.	C	B
5.	Last year, Mrs. Sue Sea won the contest.	E	V
6.	dr. Finn places the head on the snowman.	A	F
7.	Chief Tooth adds a carrot, some coal, and a scarf.	S	L
8.	Their friend, ms. Sally Shark, comes to cheer for them.	M	I
9.	The judge, Mr. Gray, looks at their snowman first.	O	W
10.	Then he and Queen White give them first prize!	T	B

What do you get when you cross a shark with a snowman?

To solve the riddle, match the circled letters to the
numbered lines below.

___ ___ ___ ___ ___ ___ ___ ___ ___ ___
6   2   9   7   1   4   8 10   5   3

Capitalization: People's titles

An Insect Invitation

Name _____ Date _____

Circle each letter that should be capitalized.

Announcing the

Bug Ball!

There will be a picnic on friday, june 30.
Be sure to join us at
555 ladybug lane
anthill, west virginia.

On saturday, july 1, we'll have a dance.
Come to
43 jitterbug Avenue
hiveboro, virginia.

Our picnic rain date is
sunday, august 4.
Don't miss the fun!

Why do the bugs need a rain date?

To solve the riddle, color each letter that you circled above.
Write the remaining letters on the lines below.

L	L	L	I	A	G	H	H	T	W	N	A	I	J	N	V	G	J	B	F	U	V	G	J	S	S	S

In case of thunder and ___ ___ ___ ___ ___ ___ ___ ___ ___ ___ ___ ___!

Sea Circus

Name _____ Date _____

Circle each letter that should be capitalized.

the Sea Circus is coming to wave town! All of the fish want to see it! Mr. and mrs. Shell shark will be there. don dolphin and will whale can't wait to get there. dr. eel wants to see the lionfish. clee Clam loves the clown fish! the swordfish act is a thrill! miss sue starfish puts on a great show! sam seal rides sea horses in the center ring. the cost of each ticket is one sand dollar. it will be a great show!

Psst! Make sure you've circled 20 letters.

Capitalization: review

Calling All Shoppers!

Name _____ Date _____

Draw a box around each letter that should be capitalized.
Write the capital letter above each box.
Color a circle that shows the same letter.

(S) (B) (S) (M) (T) (B) (E) (M) (C) (T)

critter elementary school

presents the

**Best-Ever
Yard Sale!**

monday, march 22

6:00–9:00

Find great deals on tim tiger's toys.

Buy a bike from betty bird.

Get comic books from carl camel.

Save on body warmers made by sam snake.

Taste pam python's freshly squeezed

orange juice.

Join us at

123 sale road

critterland, colorado.

(P) (C) (C) (S) (P) (S) (C) (R) (C)

With a Cherry on Top?

Name _____ Date _____

If the sentence is complete, add a period in the ☐ .
Color the cherry red.

Remember that a **complete sentence** has a subject and a verb.

1 Pam loves ice cream ☐

2 The ice cream ☐

3 She loves to eat cherries ☐

4 The whipped cream ☐

5 Nuts on a sundae taste good ☐

6 It is fun to make sundaes ☐

7 Pam likes pink sprinkles ☐

8 The spoon ☐

9 Pam wants a sundae today ☐

For each incomplete sentence, write its number in a cherry below.
On the line, rewrite the sentence so that it is complete.
Add a period.

_____

_____

_____

©The Education Center, Inc. • *Target Reading & Writing Success* • TEC60874 • Key p. 127

24 Ending Punctuation: Periods

Looking for the Loot

Name _____ Date _____

Add a period if the sentence is complete.
Reveal the path by coloring each box that has a period.

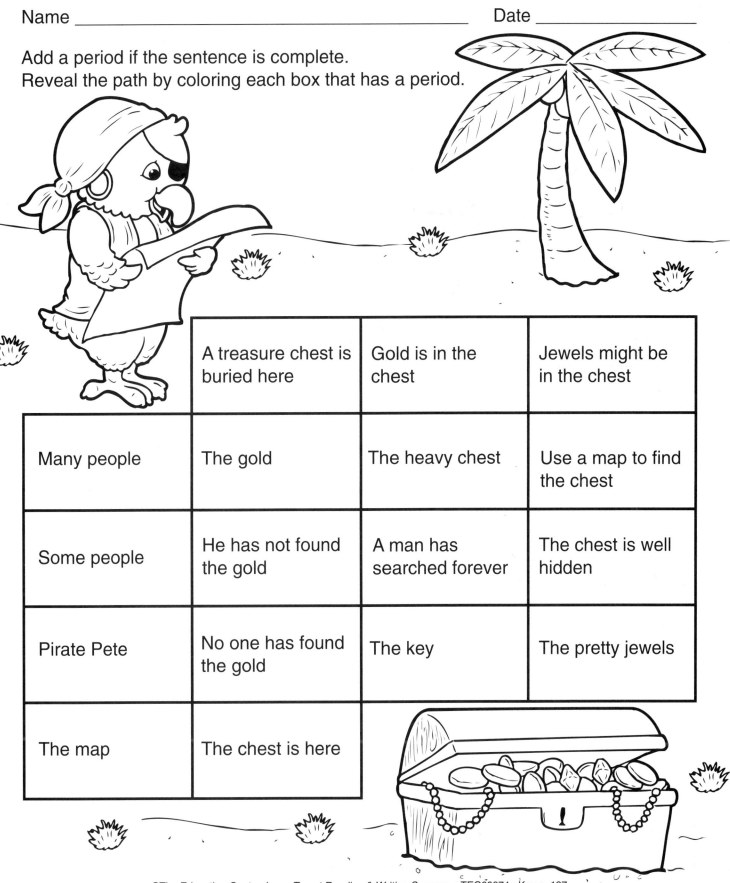

	A treasure chest is buried here	Gold is in the chest	Jewels might be in the chest
Many people	The gold	The heavy chest	Use a map to find the chest
Some people	He has not found the gold	A man has searched forever	The chest is well hidden
Pirate Pete	No one has found the gold	The key	The pretty jewels
The map	The chest is here		

Off and Running

Name _____   Date _____

Add a period or question mark in each ☐ .
Use the code to draw an X on the matching number of blank spaces.

Code	
.	= 1 space
?	= 2 spaces

START

1. Does the farmer know Ace is out of the barn ☐
2. Where is Ace going ☐
3. Ace runs through a field ☐
4. Ace runs very fast ☐
5. He wants carrots from the garden ☐
6. Will the farmer get mad ☐
7. Where is the farmer going ☐
8. Here he comes now ☐
9. Is he walking very fast ☐
10. The farmer laughs at Ace ☐
11. How many carrots did Ace get ☐
12. Ace and the farmer walk back to the barn ☐

Ending Punctuation: Periods, Question marks

Cool Kangaroo School

Name _____ Date _____

Add a period or question mark to the end of each sentence.
Color a matching eraser.

1. Most kangaroos have large ears
2. Baby kangaroos are called joeys
3. Does the baby live in the mom's pouch
4. Can a kangaroo grow over six feet tall

| . | . | ? | ? |

5. Where do kangaroos live
6. They have tails
7. What do kangaroos eat
8. Most of them eat plants

| . | ? | ? | . |

9. Kangaroos can move fast
10. What is a group of kangaroos called
11. A large group of them is called a mob
12. Are some kangaroos red

| . | ? | . | ? |

Craving Carrots

Name _____ Date _____

If the ending punctuation is correct, circle the letter in the yes column.
If the ending punctuation is not correct, circle the letter in the no column.

Yes	No	
U	D	1. Do you like to eat carrots?
J	E	2. Carrots taste great?
R	V	3. Are they easy to grow?
H	C	4. Some people eat them raw.
K	H	5. Do you like cooked carrots.
R	T	6. Does carrot cake taste good?
B	N	7. Rabbits love to eat carrots.
L	A	8. Carrots grow from small seeds?
M	S	9. How long does it take for them to grow.
T	B	10. Carrots are orange.
U	X	11. They are eaten as vegetables.
I	Q	12. Where do carrots grow?

What does a rabbit use to brush its hair?

To solve the riddle, match the letters that are circled to the numbered lines below.

___ ___   ___ ___ ___ ___   ___   " ___ ___ ___ ___ "   ___ ___ ___ ___ ___ ___ !
12 10   11 9 2 9   8   5 8 6 2   7 3 1 9 4

©The Education Center, Inc. • *Target Reading & Writing Success* • TEC60874 • Key p. 128

Ending Punctuation: Periods, Question marks

Buying a Great Book

Name _____ Date _____

Add a period or a question mark in each ☐.

CHECKOUT

1. Walt visits the bookstore ☐

2. There are a lot of books on the shelves ☐

3. Where are books about worms ☐

4. Those books are on the top shelf ☐

5. Can Walt reach those books ☐

6. Does the store have books about apples ☐

7. There are five apple books in the store ☐

8. What kind of books about soil are in the store ☐

9. Will Walt buy a book about gardens ☐

10. The garden book is on sale ☐

11. What other books are on sale ☐

12. The store is closing soon ☐

13. What book did Walt buy ☐

14. He bought *Wiggle Workouts for Worms* ☐

15. Walt carries his book home ☐

Race to the Finish

Name _____ Date _____

Who will win the race?
Color the flag if the ending punctuation is correct.

An **exclamation mark** shows strong feeling.

⚑ Tom and Tess Turtle like to ski.	⚑ They like to ski at Mount Hard Shell.
⚑ Look out for the ice.	⚑ Wow, there is 30 feet of snow!
⚑ Tess went down the slope.	⚑ What a steep mountain.
⚑ Oh, how the turtles love to ski!	⚑ Tom rides the ski lift.
⚑ The turtles wear warm clothes!	⚑ Tom tries to ski fast.
⚑ Hurry up.	⚑ Oh no, Tom fell!
⚑ Tom and Tess want to rest.	⚑ Boy, this was a great day!

Finish	Finish

Count the flags to find out who wins the race. _____

©The Education Center, Inc. • *Target Reading & Writing Success* • TEC60874 • Key p. 128

Ending Punctuation: Periods, exclamation marks

Peacock's Painting

Name _____ Date _____

Color to show the missing punctuation.

1. Pearl likes to paint

2. She painted a picture

3. Can you guess what she painted

4. She painted a peacock

5. Wow, the painting is nice

6. Did Pearl clean up

7. She washed the brushes

8. Did she clean the paint cups

9. Oh no, she forgot to clean the cups

10. She cleaned the floors and the walls

11. Did Pearl get paint on them

12. Boy, Pearl made a mess

Shh! Snakes Sleeping

Name _____   Date _____

Add the missing punctuation in each ☐.
Color each quilt patch by the code.

Are all the snakes asleep ☐	Oh no, one snake is still awake ☐	They are under a blanket ☐
Wow, they were up until 11:00 ☐	They watched a good movie ☐	Do snakes snore ☐
What time do snakes go to bed ☐	Oh my, they stayed up late ☐	The three snakes are in one bed ☐
Gee, that one snake snores loudly ☐	They will sleep well tonight ☐	What do snakes dream about ☐

Bowling a Perfect Score!

Name _____   Date _____

Write the correct punctuation on the bowling pin.
Use the code to color each bowling ball.

Color Code

. = (hatched circle)   ? = (half-filled circle)   ! = (filled circle)

1. Where do you go to bowl

2. Wow, over 100 million people bowl each year

3. Have you ever gone bowling

4. A ball is used to knock pins down

5. What is it called when all the pins fall

6. When all the pins fall down, it's called a strike

7. Do some balls weigh over 15 pounds

8. A score of 300 is the best score

9. Wow, it is hard to score 300

10. Boy, bowling balls are heavy

11. Would you like to go bowling

12. Gee, I would love to go bowling

The Doctor Is In

Name _____ Date _____

Add the missing punctuation in each ☐.
For each punctuation mark that you add, color a matching bandage.

Welcome to the office of Dr. Dragon ☐ Oh my, we are sorry you do not feel well ☐ Please come in and sit down ☐ Where do you hurt ☐ How does your throat feel ☐ Please stick out your tongue ☐ Does your head hurt ☐ Let's check to see if you have a fever ☐ Do your ears hurt ☐ Let's look in your ears ☐ Boy, you sure are a good patient, Danny ☐ We know you will get well soon ☐

Ending Punctuation: review

Flipping for Photos

Name _____ Date _____

If a comma is used correctly, circle it.
If a comma is not used correctly, cross it out.
Add a comma in the corrrect place.

1. January 4, 2005

2. March 27, 2005

3. April, 5 2005

4. June 10 2006,

5. July 8, 2006

6. August, 17 2007

7. September, 30 2007

8. October 12, 2008

9. November 1 2008,

10. December, 14 2008

A Busy Schedule

Copy each date.
Add a comma in the correct place.

1. March 8 2005

_____

2. January 31 2007

_____

3. October 14 2006

_____

4. July 11 2007

_____

5. December 20 2005

_____

6. February 7 2006

_____

7. May 23 2005

_____

8. August 2 2006

_____

9. April 13 2007

_____

10. November 30 2005

_____

11. September 17 2006

_____

12. June 28 2005

_____

Commas: dates

Boning Up!

Name _____ Date _____

If a comma is used correctly, color
  a dog bone.
If a comma is not used correctly,
  cross it out.
Add a comma in the correct place.

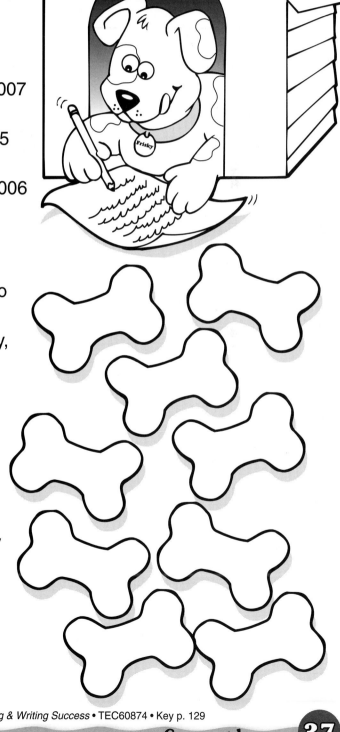

Date

1. January, 4 2005   4. June 15, 2007

2. August 20, 2006   5. July 9, 2005

3. May 26 2006,   6. March, 3 2006

Greeting

7. Dear, Rover   10. Dear, Ringo

8. , Dear Spot   11. Dear Sassy,

9. Dear Max,   12. Dear Jack,

Closing

13. Your, friend   16. With love,

14. Best wishes,   17. Yours, truly

15. , Love   18. Sincerely,

A Blossoming Writer

Name _____   Date _____

Write each friendly letter part in the correct box.
Add commas where needed.

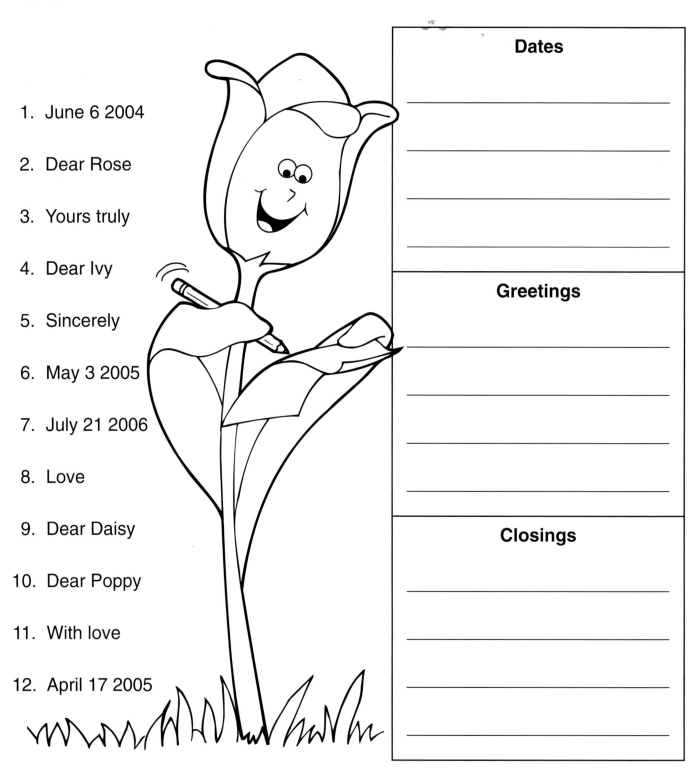

1. June 6 2004

2. Dear Rose

3. Yours truly

4. Dear Ivy

5. Sincerely

6. May 3 2005

7. July 21 2006

8. Love

9. Dear Daisy

10. Dear Poppy

11. With love

12. April 17 2005

Dates

_____

_____

_____

_____

Greetings

_____

_____

_____

_____

Closings

_____

_____

_____

_____

Saluting State Flags

Name _____   Date _____

Use the flags to match each city and state.
Write each city and state on a line below.

Remember to use a comma between the city and state.

Cities	States
Denver	South Carolina
Salt Lake City	Rhode Island
Juneau	Tennessee
Columbia	Alabama
Montgomery	Texas
Olympia	Colorado
Providence	Washington
Santa Fe	Utah
Austin	New Mexico
Nashville	Alaska

_____   _____

_____   _____

_____   _____

_____   _____

_____   _____

From Coast to Coast

Name _____ Date _____

Add commas where needed.

1. Pete Pig lives in Pink Town Maine.

2. He drove to Sausage Land Vermont, to see Pearl Pig.

3. In Pork City New York, he spent a day at the zoo.

4. He ate soybean salad in Pork Town Ohio.

5. He stopped in Baconville Kansas, and bought corn.

6. In Swine City Colorado, Pete camped in the mountains.

7. Finally, he arrived in Ham City Utah.

8. Pete and Pearl drove to Pen Village Oregon.

9. They watched whales in Porkville Oregon.

10. On his way home, Pete drove through Sty Texas.

11. Then he spent a night in Chop City Georgia.

12. He was glad to get home to Pink Town Maine!

Commas: city and state

Buggy About Mail!

Name _____   Date _____

If the comma is in the correct place, color
   the stamp.
If the comma is not in the correct place,
   cross it out.
Add a comma in the correct place.

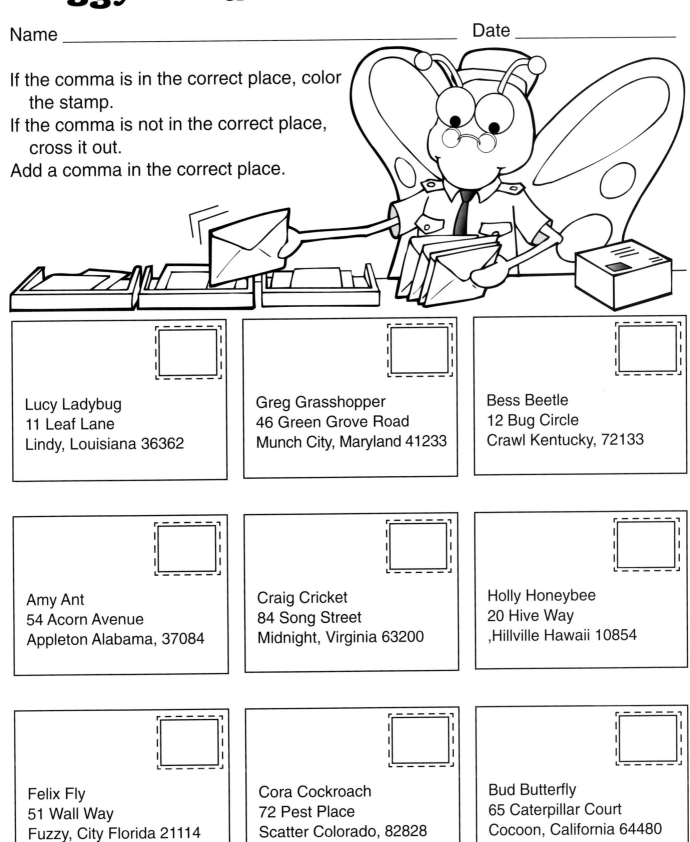

Lucy Ladybug
11 Leaf Lane
Lindy, Louisiana 36362

Greg Grasshopper
46 Green Grove Road
Munch City, Maryland 41233

Bess Beetle
12 Bug Circle
Crawl Kentucky, 72133

Amy Ant
54 Acorn Avenue
Appleton Alabama, 37084

Craig Cricket
84 Song Street
Midnight, Virginia 63200

Holly Honeybee
20 Hive Way
,Hillville Hawaii 10854

Felix Fly
51 Wall Way
Fuzzy, City Florida 21114

Cora Cockroach
72 Pest Place
Scatter Colorado, 82828

Bud Butterfly
65 Caterpillar Court
Cocoon, California 64480

Planning the Perfect Party

Name _____   Date _____

Use a red crayon to underline the first item
   in each series.
Use a blue crayon to underline the second
   item in each series.
Use a green crayon to underline the third
   item in each series.
Add commas to each sentence.

1. Tim Trudy and Tom are having a party.

2. They need to plan the food games and decorations.

3. Tim will bring hot dogs chips and sodas.

4. Trudy will buy a cake ice cream and fudge.

5. Tom will bring balloons streamers and funny hats.

6. Jen Jack and Jill come to the party.

7. The friends play cards board games and bingo.

8. Tim Jen and Jack sing a song.

9. Trudy Tom and Jill clap for their friends.

10. Food friends and games make the party a success!

Commas: items in a series

Shopping for School

Name _____ Date _____

Complete each sentence by copying
  the words from the list.
Add commas and the word *and*
  where needed.

CLOTHES
• shirts
• pants
• socks

Moe will buy _____

_____ to wear to school.

SUPPLIES
• pencils
• paper
• pens

At the school supply store, Moe will buy _____

_____ .

FOOD
• apples
• crackers
• cheese

Moe shops for _____

_____ to put in his lunchbox.

SNACKS
• bagels
• chips
• grapes

He also buys _____

_____ to eat after school.

Filling Her Free Time

Name _____ Date _____

Unscramble each group of words to form a sentence.
Write the sentence on the lines.
Add commas where needed.

1. bake to likes read Kate paint and

   _____

   _____

2. and green are best likes blue she Red colors the

   _____

   _____

3. muffins can She cookies bake and cakes

   _____

   _____

4. mystery and likes poetry books read to joke She

   _____

   _____

5. hobbies Kate interesting her and fun thinks exciting are

   _____

   _____

Commas: items in a series

From My Pad to Yours

Name _____ Date _____

Add commas where needed.

March 9 2006

Dear Fran

How are you? I am fine. I have been keeping busy. During the day, I croak hop and watch flies. At night, I sing play and clean my lily pad.

I am writing to ask you to go on a trip with me. I will be going to Hopp City Florida, on May 15 2006. I would like to stay until May 21 2006. On the way home, we can stop in Leap Town Georgia, to visit with Frank. It will be a lot of fun! Please let me know if you want to go with me by May 5 2006.

I will look forward to hearing from you!

Your friend

Fred

Commas: review 45

Track and Field Champ

Name _____ Date _____

Add commas where needed.

1. Otto loves to run jump and compete in relay races.

2. He trains at the gym in Feather City Texas.

3. At the gym, he lifts weights runs laps and does jumping jacks.

4. Otto set a high jump record on March 16 2004.

5. He was at a meet in Tall Town Texas.

6. Otto has also set records in the long jump the 500-yard dash and the mile run.

7. His next meet is on June 20 2004.

8. He will go to Longneck New Mexico, for the meet.

9. His teammates, Oscar Ollie and Opal, will go too.

10. Otto hopes to keep setting records making friends and having fun!

An ostrich has long legs. How many feet can an ostrich cover in one step?
To answer the question, count the commas you added above.

_____ feet!

Chatty Campers

Name _____ Date _____

If the quotation marks are correct, color the acorn in the yes column.

If the quotation marks are incorrect, color the acorn in the no column.

	Yes	No
1. "Sue said," Here's a great place to set up the tent.	N	G
2. "Do you need help?" asked Seth.	W	C
3. "I can do it, "answered" Sue.	A	K
4. "I'll get some sticks, Seth suggested."	H	S
5. "Great idea!" Sue replied.	Y	B
6. Seth asked, "What's that noise?	O	J
7. "You're just hearing things," Sue said.	P	T
8. I think it's a wolf! Seth "shouted."	R	U
9. "It's just the wind howling! Sue" said, laughing.	E	I

What's a squirrel's favorite food?

To solve the riddle, match each letter that is **not** colored to a numbered line below.

___ ___ ___ ___ ___   ___ ___   ___ ___ ___   ___ ___ ___
 3   2   6   8   1   6   1   7   4   9   2   6   5

Bird's-Eye View

Name _____   Date _____

Underline the speaker's exact words.
Add quotation marks.

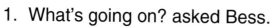

1. What's going on? asked Bess.

2. A new family just moved in, said Bertie.

3. Bess asked, Which house?

4. The one on the corner, Bertie replied.

5. I wonder whether they have any children, Bess said.

6. They don't, Bertie told her. But they have a cat.

7. Oh, no! Bess said, groaning.

8. Don't worry, Bertie said. He'll never climb up here.

9. Are you sure? Bess asked.

10. Trust me! Bertie replied.

Sleepless Sheep

Name _____ Date _____

Add any missing commas.
Each time you add a comma, color one of the stars.

1. Shawn whispered to Sheldon "Are you still awake?"

2. "Yes" Sheldon answered. "I can't sleep."

3. "You can try drinking warm milk" Shawn suggested.

4. "I don't like milk" Sheldon replied.

5. Shawn asked "Would you like for me to sing to you?"

6. "No" Sheldon said sadly.

7. Shawn said "You can count sheep."

8. Sheldon shouted "That's a great idea!"

9. Shawn warned "Just count quietly so that I can sleep!"

10. "I will" Sheldon replied. "Good night!"

Alien Arrival

Name _____ Date _____

Insert a **?**, **!**, **.**, or **,** in each ▢.
Then add quotation marks to each sentence to show the speaker's exact words.

1. Are we there yet ▢ Ork asked ▢

2. Yes! Come with me ▢ said Zorf.

3. Sert looked down and asked ▢ What's that green stuff ▢

4. That's grass ▢ Zorf replied.

5. Wow ▢ Sert yelled ▢

6. Look at all the humans ▢ Ork said, amazed.

7. Why do they only have two legs ▢ Sert asked ▢

8. Well ▢ Zorf said ▢ it's because they only have two shoes.

9. How strange ▢ Ork exclaimed.

10. Sert smiled and said ▢ We must be smarter than them!

Quotations: commas, ending punctuation

Fancy Footwork

Name _____ Date _____

Read each bug's words.
Write a sentence for each bug, putting the words in quotation marks and naming
   each speaker.
The first one has been done for you.

1. *"Would you like to dance?" asked Bernie.* _____

2. _____

3. _____

4. _____

5. _____

6. _____

Quick on Their Feet!

Name _____ Date _____

In each sentence, circle the item that is owned.
Add an apostrophe to the underlined word to show ownership.
The first one has been done for you.

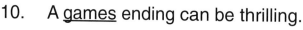

1. The <u>team's</u> (jerseys) are red.

2. The <u>skunks</u> team is fast.

3. Each <u>players</u> stick is orange.

4. Each <u>coachs</u> team plays hard.

5. The <u>goalies</u> gloves are large.

6. The <u>referees</u> whistle is loud!

7. The <u>rinks</u> ice makes skating smoother.

8. The <u>crowds</u> cheering helps the team.

9. Each <u>mascots</u> costume is silly.

10. A <u>games</u> ending can be thrilling.

Showstoppers

Name _____   Date _____

Match the symbols to find out which things belong to which animals.
Write the matching words on the lines.
Add an apostrophe where needed to show ownership.
The first one has been done for you.

☑ sharks' swimsuits

◢ _____

⊡ _____

⊙ _____

⊠ _____

⊟ _____

◸ _____

⊟ _____

△ _____

♡ _____

Animals	**Things**
⧄ sharks	◣ shoes
◢ cats	⠇ shorts
⊡ pigs	△ scarves
⊙ rabbits	◤ bows
⊠ dogs	⊟ purses
⠇ monkeys	♡ shirts
◥ horses	• pants
⊟ gerbils	⧄ swimsuits
△ snakes	⊠ hats
♡ birds	⊙ jewelry

Crazy for Toys

Name _____   Date _____

Add **'s** or **s'** to show ownership.
The first one has been done for you.

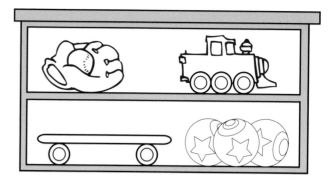

1. two monkey_s_' store

2. a toy___ price

3. one skateboard___ wheels

4. those puzzle___ pieces

5. four doll___ clothes

6. a game___ board

7. Moe___ trains

8. those toy___parts

9. that book___ pages

10. a monkey___ hat

11. five train___ cars

12. a few kid___ books

Apostrophes: singular and plural possessive nouns

Betty's Garden

Name _____   Date _____

Add **'s** or **s'** to show ownership.
Write each phrase in the correct column.
The first one has been done for you.

Singular

Plural

the gardener's hat   _____

_____   _____

_____   _____

_____   _____

                        _____

                        _____

the gardener_'s_ hat

Betty____ garden

two bird____ beaks

three ladybug____ wings

these bucket____ handles

one dog____ collar

those shovel____ handles

those flower____ petals

a garden____ plants

many plant____ leaves

Apostrophes: singular and plural possessive nouns   55

Going on a Picnic!

Name _____   Date _____

Write a contraction for each word pair.
Color the plate that shows the letter or letters that the apostrophe replaces.

ha	1.	they + will	=	_____
	2.	I + would	=	_____
o	3.	do + not	=	_____
	4.	he + will	=	_____
i	5.	we + are	=	_____
	6.	have + not	=	_____
a	7.	is + not	=	_____
	8.	she + is	=	_____
ha	9.	I + have	=	_____
	10.	we + would	=	_____
o	11.	let + us	=	_____
	12.	they + are	=	_____
a	13.	it + is	=	_____
	14.	you + have	=	_____
woul	15.	I + am	=	_____
	16.	we + have	=	_____

Right column plates: wi, o, i, u, ha, wi, a, woul

Something Fishy!

Name _____   Date _____

Use the numbers on each fish to find two
  words on the igloo.
Write the words as a contraction on the
  first line below the fish.
On the second line, write the letter(s)
  replaced by the apostrophe.
The first one has been done for you.

1. have   2. she
3. would   4. should   5. do
6. he   7. will   8. not
9. we   10. has
11. it   12. is

A.
9 3

___we'd___

___woul___

B.
4 1

_____

_____

C.
6 3

_____

_____

D.
2 7

_____

_____

E.
3 1

_____

_____

F.
9 7

_____

_____

G.
11 12

_____

_____

H.
10 8

_____

_____

I.
5 8

_____

_____

Busy Bees!

Name _____   Date _____

Write the two words that form each contraction on the lines below.
Circle the letters that the apostrophe replaced.
The first one has been done for you.

1. I've
2. haven't
3. we'd
4. they'll
5. he's
6. they're
7. doesn't
8. don't
9. couldn't
10. you've
11. I'm
12. she'd
13. it'll
14. you'll
15. we're
16. can't

1. I (have)
2. _____
3. _____
4. _____
5. _____
6. _____
7. _____
8. _____

9. _____
10. _____
11. _____
12. _____
13. _____
14. _____
15. _____
16. _____

Apostrophes: contractions

Grammar & Usage

Grammar & Usage
Table of Contents

Parent Communication and Student Checkups

*See pages 112–123 for corresponding parent communication and student checkups (mini tests) for the skills listed above.

Bunches of Books

Name _____ Date _____

Color the books that have nouns.
Write each noun on the correct book at the bottom.

A **noun** is a person, place, or thing.

| Mom | bookstore | happy | books | spider | sister | crawled |

| Spinner City | Sam Spider | tall | New York | July | go | web | fun | slow | Wally Webber | library |

People

_____ _____

_____ _____

Places

_____ _____

_____ _____

Things

_____ _____

_____ _____

Nouns: common, proper

The Race Is On!

Name _____   Date _____

Underline each proper noun.
Decide which type of noun it is.
Circle the correct letter.

	Person	Place	Thing
1. Welcome to Frogtown!	S	R	N
2. This year's jumping contest takes place on Friday.	A	L	P
3. The frogs begin on Elm Street.	C	I	B
4. Fran cheers from the stands.	S	L	E
5. The frogs have been training since May.	O	J	I
6. Fern takes the lead!	E	H	F
7. Flo is trying to keep up.	N	D	G
8. She passes Frank on the corner.	T	R	U
9. The race ends on High Street.	V	M	C
10. The winner will compete in the finals on Sunday.	B	L	G

When is the best time for a frog jumping contest?

To solve the riddle, match the circled letters
   to the numbered lines below.

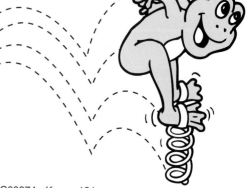

___ ___ ___ ___ ___ ___ ___ ___ ___ ___
 4   2   1   3   7   10 8   5   9   6

Nouns: proper

Surf's Up!

Name _____ Date _____

Write each noun below the correct picture.
Cross out each word as you use it.

1. _____   _____

2. _____   _____

3. _____   _____

4. _____   _____

5. _____   _____

6. _____   _____

7. _____   _____

8. _____   _____

pail	crab	crab	shell
shovel	shell	shovel	pails
crabs	pails	pail	shovels
shells	shovels	crabs	shells

BEACH

Homeward Bound

Name _____ Date _____

Add **-s** or **-es** to make each word plural.
Help Max find the path home.
Color the nine words ending in **-es.**

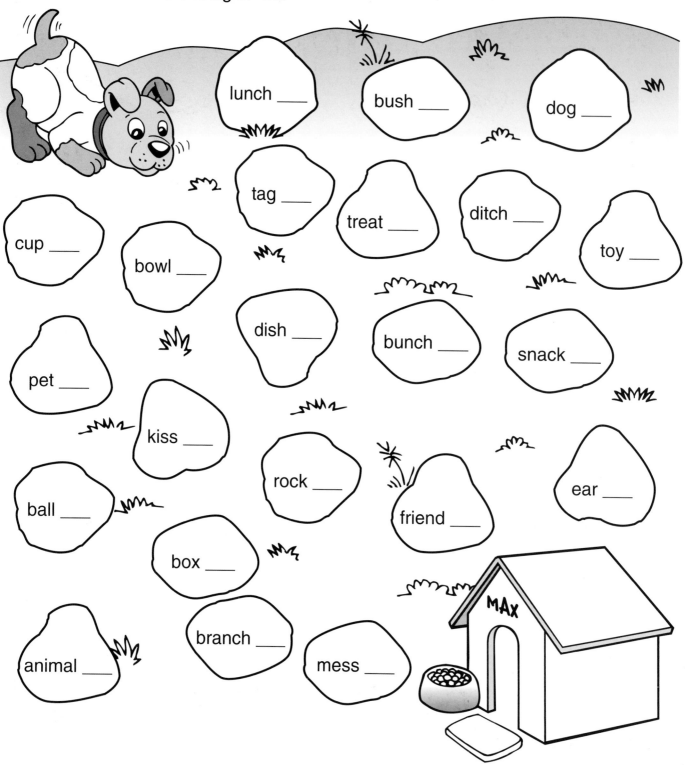

lunch ____ bush ____ dog ____

tag ____ treat ____ ditch ____ toy ____

cup ____ bowl ____ dish ____ bunch ____ snack ____

pet ____ kiss ____ rock ____ ear ____

ball ____ friend ____

box ____

animal ____ branch ____ mess ____ MAX

Nouns: plural

Two Fishy Friends

Name _____   Date _____

Make each word plural.
The first one has been done for you.

There are five words that end with **-ies.**

box **boxes** _____   sky _____

sandwich _____   wish _____

city _____   baby _____

bush _____   glass _____

party _____   family _____

Complete each sentence with a word you made.

1. Frank drinks five _____ of saltwater soda each day.

2. His friend Fran packs seaweed _____ in her lunchbox.

3. They go to birthday _____ together.

4. Frank _____ he could go on a trip.

5. Fran wants to swim to big _____ like New York City and Boston.

Fire Attire

Name _____   Date _____

Write a possessive noun to show whom
  each item belongs to.
Use the word bank.
The first one has been done for you.

Word Bank

coat   air tank
gloves   helmet
boots   pants

1. Don

   __Don's__   __coat__

2. Amy

   _____   _____

3. Sue

   _____   _____

4. Jake

   _____   _____

5. Hal

   _____   _____

6. Gus

   _____   _____

Now use the nouns you wrote above to complete the sentences.

7. _____ _____ protect his feet.

8. _____ _____ keep her legs safe from the flames.

9. _____ _____ gives him fresh air to breathe.

10. _____ _____ is buttoned up all the way.

11. _____ _____ keep his fingers from getting burned.

12. _____ _____ protects her head from harm.

©The Education Center, Inc. • *Target Reading & Writing Success* • TEC60874 • Key p. 131
Nouns: singular possessive

Play Ball!

Name _____   Date _____

Circle the nouns in each sentence.
For each noun pair, write a phrase that shows possession.
The first one has been done for you.

1. The (teams) have (coaches).
2. The players wear uniforms.
3. The uniforms have bright colors.
4. The pitchers have strong arms.
5. The players wear hats.
6. Both dugouts have benches.
7. The outfielders wear gloves.
8. Both catchers have masks.
9. The umpires have loud voices.
10. Both teams use bats.

1. _teams' coaches_ _____

2. _____

3. _____

4. _____

5. _____

6. _____

7. _____

8. _____

9. _____

10. _____

What's for Lunch?

Name _____   Date _____

Find the action verb in each row.
Color the box to reveal the path
   to the monster's lunch.

1.	the	green	lake	eat
2.	paper	dog	grab	friend
3.	tree	pack	car	pot
4.	blue	bake	pencil	street
5.	dig	coat	apple	dirt
6.	think	pizza	slow	pretty
7.	wise	save	food	orange
8.	popcorn	soda	run	house
9.	nice	puddle	soft	draw
10.	dark	yes	stir	what

Hair Ball
Salad

Monster
Flakes

Trash on Toast

Bug Soup

Lights! Camera! Action!

Name _____ Date _____

Write three action verbs that might happen at each place.
Do not use a verb more than once.

Playground

_____
_____
_____

Backyard

_____
_____
_____

Kitchen

_____
_____
_____

Bedroom

_____
_____
_____

Beach

_____
_____
_____

Classroom

_____
_____
_____

Word Wise

Name _____   Date _____

Underline the action verb in each book title.
Think of a different action verb.
On the matching line, write the new title.
The first one has been done for you.

Help me think of new book titles.

Possible Titles
1. <u>Soar</u> Through the Sky
2. Always Laugh Every Day
3. Flap Your Wings
4. Owl Loves His Tree
5. Hootie Flies Home
6. Hear the Music
7. Hootie Makes Dinner
8. Hoot in the Rain
9. Owl Saves the Forest
10. Clean Your Feathers

Other Title Ideas

1. <u>Fly Through the Sky</u>
2. _____
3. _____
4. _____
5. _____
6. _____
7. _____
8. _____
9. _____
10. _____

What a Cute Baby!

Name _____ Date _____

If the underlined word is a linking verb, lightly color
 the bib in the yes column.
If the underlined word is not a linking verb, lightly color
 the bib in the no column.
Then circle the linking verb in the sentence.

	Yes	No
1. I am in the kitchen with my mom.	I	M
2. Sam, the baby snake, is hungry.	P	A
3. Sam was not happy.	O	L
4. Sam and his sister were loud.	S	V
5. We were ready for lunch.	N	T
6. The food is on the stove.	E	K

	Yes	No
7. The plates are on the table.	B	J
8. There was plenty of food.	H	T
9. We are good eaters.	Y	G
10. The food was tasty!	R	D
11. Sam and I are full.	C	F
12. Our mom is a good cook.	Q	T

How can you tell if a snake is a baby?

To solve the riddle, match the letters in the colored bibs to the numbered lines below.

___ ___   ___ ___ ___   ___ ___ ___ ___ ___ ___ !
7   9   1   8   4   10 2 12 5   3   6

Castles by Crabs

Name _____   Date _____

Underline the verb in each sentence.
Color by the code.

1. Carl and Carla are friends.

2. This pair is very smart.

3. The crabs were at the beach.

4. The crabs build a sand castle.

5. The wet sand is heavy.

6. The pails are full of wet sand.

7. Carl finds shells for the castle.

8. Carla was in the water.

9. The ocean is rough today.

10. The water is near the castle.

11. The crabs are careful.

12. Everyone loves the castle.

Welcome!

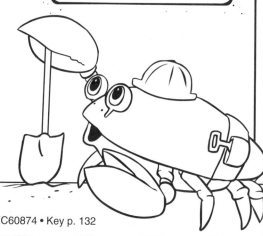

Now Playing

Name _____ Date _____

Circle the verb in each sentence.
If the verb is in present tense, color the popcorn piece
   with the matching number yellow.
If the verb is not in present tense, color the popcorn
   piece with the matching number orange.

A present tense verb tells something that is happening now.

1. Rex loves to go to the movies.

2. He wants to see *Finding Deeno.*

3. He asked his friend to go with him.

4. Rex wonders what time the movie starts.

5. He drove to the movie.

6. Rex paid for his ticket.

7. He sits in the front row.

8. The popcorn smells good.

9. Rex buys a snack.

10. Rex laughs during the movie.

11. He sat for two hours.

12. Rex clapped at the end of the movie.

13. He thought the movie was great.

14. Rex wants to see the movie again.

Fly-by-Night News

Name _____ Date _____

Circle each verb.
Write the past tense form
   of each verb on the line.

1. Sheriff Batwings calls a press conference. _____

2. Mayor Fangs plants trees on the new highway. _____

3. The Bats score two home runs. _____

4. The school closes due to snow. _____

5. The Bat Scouts thank the town for its support. _____

6. The new mall opens on Friday. _____

7. The police chase two bats from a store. _____

8. The famous singer Batty Bat visits Batville. _____

9. The Batville Fair starts today. _____

10. A bat crashes into a tree. _____

11. The police search for stolen insects. _____

12. Firefighters pull three bats from a burning tree. _____

On Top of the World

Name _____ Date _____

Color the rock beside each sentence that has a future tense verb.

A future tense verb tells something that will happen.

1. Mort Moose will climb Rocky Ridge today.

2. He bought new shoes.

3. Mort will use his own ropes.

4. He will need a new helmet.

5. The top of the rock sits up very high.

6. Mort will help his friend Mac.

7. Mort tells Mac about the trail.

8. The friends will have a great time today!

Write the future tense of each verb that is below the line.

9. Mort _____ on his helmet.
　　　　　　　put

10. It _____ an hour to climb to the top.
　　　　　take

11. Mort _____ to the top.
　　　　　　climb

12. Mort _____ to everyone.
　　　　　　wave

Crocodile Rock

Name _____ Date _____

Color each picture.
Write four adjectives that describe each picture.
Use each adjective only once.

Adjectives that tell what kind

Snail Mail

Name _____ Date _____

Write each adjective from the word bank below the correct picture.

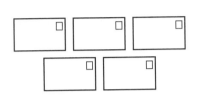

1. _____

Word Bank
two
some
ten

2. _____

3. _____

Write about the picture.
Use each adjective in a sentence.

4. many _____

_____

5. more _____

_____

6. most _____

_____

7. three _____

_____

Deep-Sea Driver

Name _____   Date _____

Rewrite each adjective, adding **-er** and **-est**.

	-er	**-est**
warm	_____	_____
fast	_____	_____
old	_____	_____
small	_____	_____
long	_____	_____
dark	_____	_____

Complete each sentence with a word you made.

1. The water feels _____ now than it did before.

2. The girl has on the _____ hat in the group.

3. The girl is _____ than the boy.

4. The driver is the _____ fish in the group.

5. The boy has _____ fins than the girl.

6. This ride is _____ than the other ride.

Hester's Hat Store

Name _____ Date _____

Add **-er** or **-est** to the adjective .

1. Hester's Hat Store is the _____ store in Pigsboro.
   (new)

2. This store has the _____ prices in town.
   (low)

3. The fur hats are the _____ hats in the store.
   (warm)

4. They are _____ than the straw hats.
   (soft)

5. The straw hats are _____ than the fur hats.
   (cheap)

6. They are also _____ than the cowboy hats.
   (small)

7. The cowboy hats are on the _____ shelf in the store.
   (high)

8. The _____ hat in the store has flowers on it.
   (wild)

9. It is _____ than the hat with the feathers.
   (tall)

10. Hester keeps her store _____ than the other hat store.
    (clean)

Martian Mall

Name _____ Date _____

Help Neroy find his way to the mall.
If the space has an adjective, color it yellow.

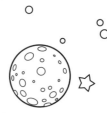

		windy	shorter	helpful
rabbit	monkey	plant	see	crunchy
drink	sunny	smaller	happy	darkest
pencil	furry	phone	grow	paint
days	many	tall	dog	park
walk	house	glad		

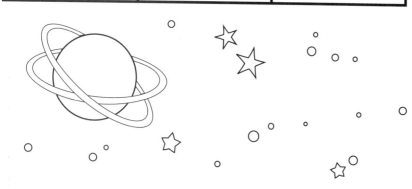

Monkeys on the Loose!

Name _____   Date _____

Circle each adjective.
Write each adjective on the chart.

1. The zoo has many playful monkeys.

2. Two monkeys got out of the large cage.

3. The monkeys let out three hungry bears.

4. One furry bear made a loud growl.

5. The zookeeper caught the five animals.

Adjectives That Tell How Many	Adjectives That Tell What Kind

A Cowpoke's Trip Into Town

Name _____ Date _____

Rewrite each sentence using two or more adjectives.
Underline each adjective with a red crayon.

1. Tex rode his horse into the town.

   _____

2. He bought a hat.

   _____

3. Tex also bought a belt.

   _____

4. He ate a bowl of chili.

   _____

5. He fed his horse carrots.

   _____

6. Then Tex rode to his home.

   _____

Getting Ready for School

Name _____ Date _____

Underline each adverb that tells how.
Write the adverb in the puzzle.

Across

3. Chip's toys are neatly put away.
6. Chip safely gets up on the bed.
8. Chip proudly shows Mom his room.
9. The family eagerly starts the day.
10. Mom gladly packs Chip's lunch.

Down

1. Dad gently shuts the door.
2. Mom quickly fixes eggs.
4. Mom tenderly pats Chip's back.
5. Chip happily dresses for school.
7. Chip sweetly thanks Mom.

Rodeo Armadillo

Name _____ Date _____

Choose the adverb that tells how.
Color the saddle orange.

1. Tex _____ gets on a bull.

2. The bull stands _____ still.

3. Tex pats the bull _____ on the head.

4. The bull _____ licks Tex.

5. Tex whistles _____.

6. The bull _____ begins to buck.

7. The crowd cheers _____.

8. Tex _____ holds on to the saddle.

9. Tex _____ calms the bull down.

10. The bull _____ walks to the fence.

11. Tex _____ thanks the bull for the ride.

12. A judge _____ gives Tex a trophy.

slowly	later
inside	perfectly
softly	above
behind	playfully
loudly	today
there	quickly
excitedly	below
here	wisely
easily	upstairs
gladly	outside
now	politely
proudly	first

Adverbs that tell how

To the Point

Name _____ Date _____

Write a sentence about each picture.
Use the adverb.

1. playfully _____

_____

2. carefully _____

_____

3. quickly _____

_____

4. neatly _____

_____

5. lovingly _____

_____

6. slowly _____

_____

Chilly's Lunch

Name _____ Date _____

In each sentence, circle the adverb that tells when.
Write the adverb in the matching space.

The Igloo Outdoor Café

(1) On his trip, Chilly unpacks first. (2) Next, he puts his golf clubs by the door. (3) He has not played golf before. (4) He ate breakfast early and needs lunch. (5) He thinks about eating later in the day. (6) Suddenly, he hears a loud sound. (7) His tummy has never growled that loud! (8) Soon he runs to the café. (9) He has only eaten there once. (10) Lunch was so good that he can't wait for dinner tonight!

1. ___ ◯ ___ ___ ___
2. ___ ◯ ___ ___
3. ◯ ___ ___ ___ ___
4. ◯ ___ ___ ___
5. ___ ___ ___ ◯ ___
6. ___ ◯ ___ ___ ___ ___
7. ___ ___ ◯ ___
8. ◯ ___ ___ ___
9. ___ ◯ ___ ___
10. ___ ___ ◯ ___

What do penguins like to eat?
To solve the riddle, match the circled letters to the numbered lines below.

___ ___ ___ ___ ___ ___ ___ ___ ___ ___
  1   9   2   3   6   7   10   4   5   8

Made in the Shade

Name _____   Date _____

Circle the adverb on each leaf that tells where.

up
today

softly
close

soon
down

inside
slowly

above
quickly

later
outside

everywhere
loudly

far
now

Complete the paragraph by writing
one circled adverb on each line.

Andy Ape goes _____ to play in the

sun. He stays _____ to the house. Andy

thinks he left his snack _____ on the

table. He looks _____ for his snack and

can't find it. He looks _____ and sees

bananas hanging in a tree. He climbs to the top of

the tree and grabs a huge banana. Then he climbs

_____ the tree and eats his new snack.

A Crowd Favorite!

Name _____ Date _____

Underline each adverb.
Color each poster by the code.

Color Code
adverbs that tell how = orange
adverbs that tell when = green
adverbs that tell where = yellow

The basketball game starts soon.

The crowd cheers loudly!

Everyone wishes Tim good luck today.

Tim ties his shoes here.

Tim is ready to start the game now.

He throws the ball up.

Tim quickly scores two points.

The crowd cheerfully claps for Tim.

TIGERS 2

Adverbs: review

Ready, Set, Go!

Name _____   Date _____

Circle each adverb.
Help Ricky Racer cross the finish line!
Connect the circles to find the path to the finish line.

START

safely   tire   quickly   now

wave   there

shiny   laugh   see

helmet   above

book

later   proudly   carefully

car   tree   tomorrow

behind   happily   next

drive   belt   sit

today   below   flag   soon

FINISH

Celebration in the Sky

Name _____   Date _____

Write a pronoun on the line to replace the underlined noun or nouns.
Use the word bank.

1. <u>The Fourth of July</u> is a fun holiday.

   _____ is a celebration of the birthday of our country.

2. <u>Sara, Adam, and I</u> are going to see the fireworks.
   My mom is driving _____.

3. The <u>fireworks</u> light up the night sky.

   _____ are amazing!

4. <u>Sara</u> doesn't like the loud ones.

   _____ plugs her ears.

5. <u>Adam</u> can watch for hours.

   _____ says it looks like a shower of colors.

6. The <u>fireworks</u> are very beautiful.
   I enjoy seeing _____ every year.

7. <u>My friends and I</u> have a great time.

   _____ think it's the best holiday of the year!

Word Bank
he
she
it
them
we
they
us

Basketball Stars

Name _____ Date _____

Write a pronoun to take the place of the underlined noun or nouns.

These pronouns can stand for a single noun.

it he she him her

These pronouns can stand for two or more nouns.

they them

1. <u>Jill and Joey</u> play on the same team. _____

2. <u>Coach Bud</u> knew it would be a great season. _____

3. Jill's family came to watch <u>the game</u>. _____

4. <u>Jill</u> was excited to play. _____

5. Jill passed the ball to <u>Joey</u>. _____

6. <u>Joey</u> scored just in time. _____

7. Joey told <u>Jill</u> that she did a good job. _____

8. <u>The game</u> lasted one hour. _____

9. <u>The players</u> were tired. _____

10. The coach was proud of <u>the players</u>. _____

Letter to a Friend

Name _____ Date _____

Write the noun or nouns that each underlined pronoun is replacing.
Use the word bank.
Some words may be used more than once.

Dear Pen Pal,

Hi! My name is Sammy. <u>I</u>[1.] am eight years old. I live with my mom and brother. <u>We</u>[2.] live in an apartment. <u>It</u>[3.] is very high in the sky! My brother and I love going to the park. <u>He</u>[4.] likes the trees. I like the benches. Sometimes I find food on <u>them</u>[5.]! Mom comes to the park with <u>us</u>[6.] when <u>she</u>[7.] is not too busy. Maybe <u>you</u>[8.] can come visit <u>me</u>[9.]! I will take <u>you</u>[10.] to the park! Please write soon.

Your friend,
Sammy

1. _____
2. _____
3. _____
4. _____
5. _____
6. _____
7. _____
8. _____
9. _____
10. _____

Word Bank
Sammy
Mom
brother
pen pal
apartment
benches

Pronouns: singular, plural

Campsite Belongings

Name _____   Date _____

Write a possessive pronoun on each line.
Use the word bank.
Some words may be used more than once.

Possessive Pronouns

my	its
his	their
her	your
our	

1. The tent belongs to me. It is _____ tent.

2. Rob owns the flashlight. It is _____ flashlight.

3. We brought the food. It is _____ food.

4. The fishing pole is Ruth's. It is _____ fishing pole.

5. Does the bug spray belong to you? Is it _____ bug spray?

6. I own the compass. It is _____ compass.

7. Do these sleeping bags belong to them? Are they _____ sleeping bags?

8. Those are Rita's pans. They are _____ pans.

9. The radio belongs to Rex. It is _____ radio.

10. The apples came from that tree. They are _____ apples.

An Ant Adventure

Name _____ Date _____

Draw a box around the possessive pronoun in each sentence.
Circle the noun or nouns to which the pronoun refers.

1. Al is walking with his friend Ann.

2. The ants see something in their path.

3. Al claps his hands.

4. Ann waves her arms.

5. Al and Ann squeal, "It is our lucky day!"

6. The ants climb inside the basket and taste its goodies.

7. A lady yells, "Get out of my basket!"

8. Al looks at his friend Ann.

9. Ann looks at her friend Al.

10. The ants run as fast as their little legs will go!

Circle each word you boxed
    in the puzzle below.

H	E	R	T	B	A
I	T	S	H	I	S
S	L	N	E	F	W
P	Q	H	I	S	H
M	O	U	R	C	E
Y	T	H	E	I	R

©The Education Center, Inc. • *Target Reading & Writing Success* • TEC60874 • Key p. 134

Moonstruck!

Name _____ Date _____

Choose the missing verb.
Color the box in the correct column.

		is	are
1.	The moon _____ over 238,000 miles away.	B	E
2.	It _____ made of rock.	F	S
3.	Craters _____ holes in the surface.	G	C
4.	Big flat areas on the moon _____ called seas.	U	L
5.	No water _____ in these seas.	M	I

		was	were
6.	People once thought the moon_____ magic.	W	D
7.	Tales _____ made up about it.	P	J
8.	One story _____ that a full moon makes you crazy.	Q	H
9.	Some said the moon _____ a bowl of fire.	K	T
10.	Myths about why coyotes howl at the moon _____ also told.	A	O

Find out what the other animals think of the coyote's moonlight singing.
For each number, write the letter you **did not** color.

___ ___ ___   ___ ___ N ___ N ___ N ___ ___ ___ ___   ___   ___ N ___ - ___ ___ ___ !
8 5 2   2 5   3   5   3   1 1 6 2   10   9 4   1   4 7

©The Education Center, Inc. • *Target Reading & Writing Success* • TEC60874 • Key p. 134

Smooth Sailing

Name _____ Date _____

If the underlined word is correct, put a ✓ by it.
If it is incorrect, put an ✗ on it.
Then write the correct word in the box.

		Dan and Deb <u>love</u> to sail.	They <u>sails</u> each day.
Dan <u>clean</u> the boat.	Deb <u>makes</u> lunch.	They <u>go</u> to the lake.	The waves <u>hits</u> the boat.
	The sun <u>shines</u> so bright.	The wind <u>blow</u> the sails.	
Dan and Deb <u>rests</u> in the sun.	Dan <u>reads</u> the paper.	He also <u>steers</u> the boat.	Deb <u>enjoy</u> a good book.
	She <u>talk</u> on the phone too.	They both <u>take</u> a swim.	Dan and Deb <u>ride</u> home.

Find Dan and Deb's course.
Color each box that has a ✓.

Up, Up, and Away!

Name _____ Date _____

Underline the subject.
Circle the correct verb in ( ).

1. (Have, Has) you ever been in a hot-air balloon?

2. Some people (like, likes) to race them.

3. Others (drift, drifts) slowly for fun.

4. Balloons (come, comes) in different sizes.

5. Warm air (make, makes) a balloon rise.

6. A large fan (blow, blows) air into the bag.

7. Then a burner (heat, heats) the air.

8. The balloon (rise, rises) slowly.

9. Passengers (ride, rides) in the basket.

10. They (go, goes) up, up, and away!

Race Day

Name _____ Date _____

For each set of flags, match each subject to a verb. Connect the black dots. Write each matching pair in a sentence.

Subjects   **Verbs**

A.
driver •   • love
fans •   • loves
_____
_____
_____

B.
crowd •   • waves
flags •   • wave
_____
_____

C.
cars •   • go
driver •   • goes
_____
_____

D.
everyone •   • smile
winners •   • smiles
_____
_____

E.
race •   • take
people •   • takes
_____
_____

©The Education Center, Inc. • *Target Reading & Writing Success* • TEC60874 • Key p. 134
Subject-verb agreement

Parent Communication and Student Checkups

Parent Communication and Student Checkups

Table of Contents

How to Administer the checkups

Both checkups can be given at the same time, or Checkup B can be given as a follow-up test for students who did not do well on Checkup A.

Student Progress Chart

student		Date	Number Correct	Comments
Checkup 1 Capitalization	A			
	B			
Checkup 2 Ending punctuation	A			
	B			
Checkup 3 Commas	A			
	B			
Checkup 4 Quotations	A			
	B			
Checkup 5 Apostrophes	A			
	B			
Checkup 6 Nouns	A			
	B			
Checkup 7 Verbs	A			
	B			
Checkup 8 Adjectives	A			
	B			
Checkup 9 Adverbs	A			
	B			
Checkup 10 Pronouns	A			
	B			
Checkup 11 Subject-verb agreement	A			
	B			

It's Time to Take Aim!

On _____ our class will be having a checkup on **capitalization.** To help your child prepare, please spend about 15 minutes reviewing this skill.

Skill Refresher

Hide the answers at the bottom of the page. Guide your child through the rules and examples below. Then have him complete problems 1–8.

- Capitalize the **first word in a sentence.**

    T
    [t]he frog went to the mall.

- Capitalize **names** and **people's titles.**

    S   J   J
    [s]ally   [j]udge [j]ody

- Capitalize the **days** of the week, **months** of the year, and **holidays.**

    W   A   P   D
    [w]ednesday   [a]ugust   [p]residents' [d]ay

- Capitalize **geographic names.**

    M   S   H   A   O
    [m]ount [s]t. [h]elens   [a]tlantic [o]cean

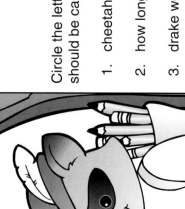

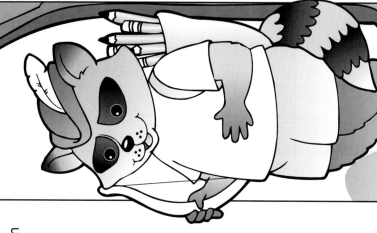

Target These!

Circle the letter or letters in each sentence that should be capitalized.

1. cheetahs are the fastest mammals on land.

2. how long can a cat's claws grow?

3. drake went to see dr. smith today.

4. I think sue is in mr. daniel's class.

5. On friday, we're going to the movies for st. patrick's day!

6. In july, we celebrate the fourth of july.

7. Jordan plans to visit the mojave desert.

8. wheeler peak is in the rocky mountains.

Answers:

1. **C**heetahs are the fastest mammals on land.
2. **H**ow long can a cat's claws grow?
3. **D**rake went to see **Dr. S**mith today.
4. I think **S**ue is in **Mr. D**aniel's class.
5. On **F**riday, we're going to the movies for **St. P**atrick's **D**ay!
6. In **J**uly, we celebrate the **F**ourth of **J**uly.
7. **J**ordan plans to visit the **M**ojave **D**esert.
8. **W**heeler **P**eak is in the **R**ocky **M**ountains.

Checkup 1

Name _____ Date _____

Circle the letter or letters in each sentence that should be capitalized.

1. lions sleep most of the day.

2. what time do we eat lunch?

3. The books belong to mr. cash.

4. d\r. jones is rick's doctor too.

5. On monday, we are going to the park for veterans day!

6. School is closed one day in january for martin luther king jr. day.

7. We will visit the pacific ocean this summer!

8. The grand canyon has cliffs, a river, and lots of rocks.

Checkup 1

Name _____ Date _____

Circle the letter or letters in each sentence that should be capitalized.

1. how old is your dog?

2. he reads ten pages each night.

3. My dentist's name is dr. nelson.

4. The art teacher is ms. price.

5. In november we have turkey for thanksgiving.

6. The fourth of july is on a friday this year!

7. There are many types of plants in asia.

8. The great lakes touch several states.

It's Time to Take Aim!

On _____ our class will be having a checkup on **ending punctuation**. To help your child prepare, please spend about 15 minutes reviewing this skill.

Skill Refresher

Hide the answers at the bottom of the page. Guide your child through the rules and examples below. Then have him complete problems 1–8.

- **A period** is used at the end of a complete sentence that is a statement. A complete sentence has a subject and a verb.

  Let's go to the movies Friday night.

- **A question mark** is used at the end of a question.

  What time do we go to lunch?

- **An exclamation mark** shows strong feeling.

  Wow, look at all of the stars in the sky!

Target These!

Add the missing punctuation.

1. I like to play outside after school

2. Oh my, we're late for the party

3. Where are the laces for my skates

4. Who left this money on the table

5. Jamie has hockey practice today at 5:00

6. Oh no, I left my homework at home

7. Why did Jorge leave early

8. Wait for me

Answers:

1. I like to play outside after school.
2. Oh my, we're late for the party!
3. Where are the laces for my skates?
4. Who left this money on the table?
5. Jamie has hockey practice today at 5:00.
6. Oh no, I left my homework at home!
7. Why did Jorge leave early?
8. Wait for me!

Checkup 2

Name _____ Date _____

Add the missing punctuation.

1. When do we leave for the circus

2. Ouch, my shoes are too tight

3. Keep out

4. What do brussels sprouts taste like

5. She would like to buy a football and a soccer ball

6. I will read my book after dinner

7. Ben will bring the cake

8. Who lives in the blue house on the corner

9. Ellie, be careful

105

Checkup 2

Name _____ Date _____

Add the missing punctuation.

1. Wow, it is really dark outside

2. Oh boy, we're having pizza for lunch

3. Where is Tony hiding

4. My favorite book is about a horse and a farm

5. Texas is in the southern United States

6. How much longer until we get there

7. Whom do these belong to

8. Hey, my friend likes Jell-O gelatin, just like I do

9. Her birthday is in May

It's Time to Take Aim!

On _____ our class will be having a checkup on **commas.**
To help your child prepare, please spend about 15 minutes reviewing this skill.

Skill Refresher

Hide the answers at the bottom of the page. Guide your child through the rules and examples below. Then have him complete problems 1–7.

- Commas are used to separate the **day** and the **year.**

  July 4, 2010   March 21, 1971

- Commas are used to separate the **city** and the **state.**

  Denver, Colorado   Austin, Texas

- Commas are used to separate **items in a series.**

  She brought pencils, paper, and books to school.

- Commas are used in letters **after the greeting and the closing.**

  Dear Barbara,   Yours truly,

Target These!

Add commas where needed.

1. The games will start on June 5 2006.

2. That happened on August 19 1852.

3. Jen and Tim went to Bismarck North Dakota, in the spring.

4. Where is Albany New York?

5. Wendy bought new shoes shirts shorts and socks for soccer practice.

6. Please bring a camera your journal and a pencil on the field trip.

7. Dear Sam
   I hope you visit soon. I miss you.
   Your pal
   Tom

4. Where is Albany, New York?
5. Wendy bought new shoes, shirts, shorts, and socks for soccer practice.
6. Please bring a camera, your journal, and a pencil on the field trip.

7. Dear Sam,
   I hope you visit soon. I miss you.
   Your pal,
   Tom

©The Education Center, Inc. • *Target Reading & Writing Success* • TEC60874

Answers:
1. The games will start on June 5, 2006.
2. That happened on August 19, 1852.
3. Jen and Tim went to Bismarck, North Dakota, in the spring.

Checkup 3

Name _____ Date _____

Add commas where needed.

1. Man first walked on the moon on July 20 1969.

2. The new space-age car will be for sale on May 3 2022.

3. She is from Key West Florida.

4. Is Atlanta Georgia, near Macon Georgia?

5. I want pizza salad fruit and a drink for lunch.

6. After school we can play games ride bikes or go to the park.

7. Dear Lee

   I hope you are having fun at camp. Write soon.

                                Your friend

                                Nick

Test A: Commas

©The Education Center, Inc. • *Target Reading & Writing Success* • TEC60874 • Key p. 135

107

Checkup 3

Name _____ Date _____

Add commas where needed.

1. Harry S. Truman was born on May 8 1884.

2. They will buy a new house on August 15 2007.

3. He lives in Ludlow Vermont.

4. How far is Salt Lake City Utah, from here?

5. We brought a tent a sleeping bag food and water on the camping trip.

6. Each night I lay out my clothes books and homework for school.

7. Dear Randy

   Thank you for your letter. I will write you a longer letter soon.

                                Your pal

                                James

Test B: Commas

©The Education Center, Inc. • *Target Reading & Writing Success* • TEC60874 • Key p. 135

It's Time to Take Aim!

108

On _____ our class will be having a checkup on **quotations**. To help your child prepare, please spend about 15 minutes reviewing this skill.

Skill Refresher

Hide the answers at the bottom of the page. Guide your child through the rules and examples below. Then have him complete sentences 1–9.

- **Quotation marks** are placed around the exact words of a speaker.

  "What time is it?" asked Tom.

- **Commas** are used to separate the speaker from the quoted words.

  Ben said, "I will be there later."

- **Periods, question marks,** and **exclamation marks** are placed inside the quotation marks to punctuate the words of the speaker.

  "Wow," John exclaimed, "I didn't know that!"

Target These!

Add quotation marks where needed.

1. I love to go to the movies, Phil said.
2. John answered, I'll be there in a few minutes.
3. Bob, whispered Jen, where are you?

Add commas where needed.

4. "My favorite kind of car is a truck" said Melanie.
5. "Yes" replied Nick, "I do like pizza."
6. Trish asked "Whose house is this?"

Add proper punctuation where needed.

7. "Is this your dog " asked Liz.
8. Bill shouted That's my cookie you're eating
9. Make a right turn" Sal said "not a left turn

Answers:

1. **"**I love to go to the movies**,"** Phil said.
2. John answered, **"**I'll be there in a few minutes.**"**
3. **"**Bob,**"** whispered Jen, **"**where are you?**"**
4. "My favorite kind of car is a truck**,**" said Melanie.
5. "Yes**,**" replied Nick, "I do like pizza."
6. Trish asked**,** "Whose house is this?"
7. "Is this your dog**?**" asked Liz.
8. Bill shouted**, "**That's my cookie you're eating**!"**
9. **"**Make a right turn**,**" Sal said, "not a left turn**."**

Checkup 4

Name _____ Date _____

Add the quotation marks where needed.

1. Pam answered, I'll clean my room right now, Mom.

2. I love to go sledding in the winter, Blake said.

3. Jan, whispered Beth, is that you?

Add commas where needed.

4. Nia asked "Is this a new bike?"

5. "No" replied Steve "I don't have your book."

6. "My favorite fruit is an orange" said Kelly.

Add proper punctuation where needed.

7. Roz shouted We're going to be late

8. "Do you want to borrow my pencil" asked Les

9. First, we went to lunch" Sal said "and then to the mall

Test A: Quotations

©The Education Center, Inc. • *Target Reading & Writing Success* • TEC60874 • Key p. 135

Checkup 4

Name _____ Date _____

Add the quotation marks where needed.

1. It is too cold to go swimming, Shelly said.

2. Lou replied, I wish I had a dog like yours.

3. Jill, whispered Ellie, are you awake?

Add commas where needed.

4. "Okay" announced Dan "it's time to go to the dentist."

5. Jeff asked "Are we going to the game this weekend?"

6. "I eat fish once a week" said Pete.

Add proper punctuation where needed.

7. May exclaimed Someone gave me a present

8. "Do ants like living underground?" wondered Raul

9. I liked the first part" Paul said "but the second part was boring

Test B: Quotations

©The Education Center, Inc. • *Target Reading & Writing Success* • TEC60874 • Key p. 135

It's Time to Take Aim!

On _____ our class will be having a checkup on **apostrophes.**
To help your child prepare, please spend about 15 minutes reviewing this skill.

Skill Refresher

Hide the answers at the bottom of the page. Guide your child through the rules and examples below. Then have him complete problems 1–8.

- Add **'s** to a singular noun to show ownership.

  Trudy**'s** sunglasses   a dog**'s** ears
  a garden**'s** soil   a car**'s** wheels

- Add **s'** to a plural noun to show ownership.

  birds**'** feathers   books**'** pages
  baskets**'** handles   trees**'** leaves

- In **contractions,** apostrophes take the place of specific letters.

  she is = she's   they are = they're
  does not = doesn't   you will = you'll

Target These!

Add **'s** or **s'** to show ownership.

1. Jon_____ ice cream
2. Mom_____ car
3. some snake_____ scales
4. many tree_____ leaves

Rewrite each word pair to make a contraction. Write the letter(s) the apostrophe replaces.

5. have not _____

6. I will _____

7. we would _____

8. let us _____

Answers:

1. Jon**'s** ice cream
2. Mom**'s** car
3. some snake**s'** scales
4. many tree**s'** leaves
5. haven't, o
6. I'll, wi
7. we'd, woul
8. let's, u

Checkup 5

Name _____ Date _____

Add **'s** or **s'** to show ownership.

1. one box____ top

2. a crab____ shell

3. the baby____ rattle

4. a few dog____ collars

5. some place____ names

6. three computer____ screens

Rewrite each word pair to make a contraction.
Write the letter(s) the apostrophe replaces.

7. they have _____ _____

8. she will _____ _____

9. should not _____ _____

10. I am _____ _____

111

Checkup 5

Name _____ Date _____

Add **'s** or **s'** to show ownership.

1. a bird____ nest

2. one writer____ pen

3. an orange____ seeds

4. two blanket____ softness

5. many spider____ legs

6. some book____ titles

Rewrite each word pair to make a contraction.
Write the letter(s) the apostrophe replaces.

7. they will _____ _____

8. he is _____ _____

9. I would _____ _____

10. has not _____ _____

It's Time to Take Aim!

On _____ our class will be having a checkup on **nouns.** To help your child prepare, please spend about 15 minutes reviewing this skill.

Skill Refresher

Hide the answers at the bottom of the page. Guide your child through the rules and examples below. Then have him complete problems 1–8.

- A **proper noun** names a special person, place, or thing.

  Jared Jones   America   September

- Make most **nouns plural** by adding **-s** or **-es** or by changing the **y** to **i** and adding **-es.**

  pencils   branches   **cities**

- A **possessive noun** shows to whom an item belongs.

  Jenny's game   book's cover
  monkeys' tails   boxes' tops

Target These!

Circle the proper nouns.

1. Jackie   town   Kansas
   sister   March   book

Rewrite each word to make it plural.

2. card _____   desk _____

3. fox _____   brush _____

4. bunny _____   penny _____

Write a phrase that shows possession. The first one has been done for you.

5. ball of Kate   _Kate's ball_

6. train of Kevin _____

7. wings of birds _____

8. shoes of boys _____

Answers:

1. Jackie, March, Kansas
2. cards, desks
3. foxes, brushes
4. bunnies, pennies
5. Kate's ball
6. Kevin's train
7. birds' wings
8. boys' shoes

©The Education Center, Inc. • *Target Reading & Writing Success* • TEC60874

Checkup 6

Name _____ Date _____

Circle the proper nouns.

1. Friday   child   France

    city   Betty   truck

Rewrite each word to make it plural.

2. cup _____ taco _____

3. glass _____ beach _____

4. pony _____ country _____

Write a phrase that shows possession. The first one has been done for you.

5. DVD of Linda _Linda's DVD_

6. skateboard of Ramon _____

7. wheels of cars _____

8. collars of dogs _____

Checkup 6

Name _____ Date _____

Circle the proper nouns.

1. school   soup   Helen Keller

    Grand Canyon   grandmother   Memorial Day

Rewrite each word to make it plural.

2. zebra _____ flower _____

3. guess _____ watch _____

4. body _____ cherry _____

Write a phrase that shows possession. The first one has been done for you.

5. headphones of Donna _Donna's headphones_

6. hamburger of Randy _____

7. ears of rabbits _____

8. seats of buses _____

It's Time to Take Aim!

On _____ our class will be having a checkup on **verbs.**
To help your child prepare, please spend about 15 minutes reviewing this skill.

Skill Refresher

Hide the answers at the bottom of the page. Guide your child through the rules and examples below. Then have him complete problems 1–8.

- An **action verb** tells what the subject is doing, has done, or will do.

  The dog **barked** at the squirrel in the tree.

- A **linking verb** links the subject to another part of the sentence.

  The bowl **is** on the table.

- The **tense of a verb** tells when it takes place.

  present: Joe **plays** on his school basketball team.
  past: Joe **played** on his school basketball team.
  future: Joe **will play** on his school basketball team.

Target These!

Circle the action verb in each sentence.

1. The squirrel runs up the tree.

2. The boy thought about the math problems.

3. She drew a picture for her teacher.

Circle the linking verb in each sentence.

4. He is nine years old.

5. They were at the mall.

Write "present," "past," or "future" to tell the tense of the underlined verb.

6. Joe <u>will swing</u> on the rope. _____

7. Kim <u>laughed</u> at the joke. _____

8. The dog <u>scratches</u> for fleas. _____

Answers:

1. runs
2. thought
3. drew
4. He(is)nine years old.
5. They(were)at the mall.
6. future
7. past
8. present

Checkup 7

Name _____ Date _____

Circle the action verb in each sentence.

1. Gene listens carefully to the words.

2. The rabbit jumped over the log.

3. She paints pictures of boats.

Circle the linking verb in each sentence.

4. The fish were in the fish tank.

5. The librarian is quiet.

Write "present," "past," or "future" to tell the tense of the underlined verb.

6. The horse <u>tipped</u> over the cart. _____

7. She <u>will bring</u> the desserts. _____

8. Lou <u>plays</u> the flute. _____

Test A: Verbs

Checkup 7

Name _____ Date _____

Circle the action verb in each sentence.

1. The boy looks for his game.

2. Shelly wondered if the toy was for sale.

3. The lion roars loudly.

Circle the linking verb in each sentence.

4. The monkeys are in the zoo.

5. The lady was in her car.

Write "present," "past," or "future" to tell the tense of the underlined verb.

6. The radio <u>will play</u> our song. _____

7. They <u>painted</u> the house green. _____

8. Sarah <u>loves</u> hamburgers. _____

Test B: Verbs

It's Time to Take Aim!

On _____ our class will be having a checkup on **adjectives**.
To help your child prepare, please spend about 15 minutes reviewing this skill.

Skill Refresher

Hide the answers at the bottom of the page. Guide your child through the rules and examples below. Then have him complete problems 1–8.

- Some adjectives tell **what kind.**

  colorful   dry   yellow
  happy   soft   wonderful
  sunny   sour

- Some adjectives tell **how many.**

  five   many   some
  more   several a lot
          few
          one

- Add *-er* or *-est* to an adjective to show a **comparison.**

  taller   newer   smallest   cheapest
  older   higher   longest   cleanest

Target These!

Circle the adjectives in each sentence.

1. The stubborn, old mule didn't want to move.

2. Tiny bugs live in the tall grass.

Write an adjective from the box beside the correct picture.

> many
> four
> six

3. _____

4. _____

5. _____

Add **-er** or **-est** to each adjective to complete the sentence.

6. The water is _____ than before.
   (high)

7. Of all the ships, those are the _____.
   (fast)

8. Chocolate cookies are the _____!
   (sweet)

Answers:

1. The (stubborn), (old) mule didn't want to move.
2. (Tiny) bugs live in the (tall) grass.

3. six
4. many

5. four
6. higher

7. fastest
8. sweetest

Checkup 8

Name _____ Date _____

Circle the adjectives in each sentence.

1. Red and yellow flowers are blooming in the garden.

2. Alex helped the scared cat and the fearful dog.

Write an adjective from the box beside the correct picture.

| couple |
| some |
| five |

3. ○○○○ _____

4. ○○ _____

5. ○○ ○○○ _____

Add **-er** or **-est** to each adjective to complete the sentence.

6. Sue is _____ than Todd. (young)

7. Jim has the _____ jacket I've seen. (cool)

8. That mountain is the _____ in the state. (high)

Checkup 8

Name _____ Date _____

Circle the adjectives in each sentence.

1. We sat on the cold, hard floor.

2. That black eagle has huge wings.

Write an adjective from the box beside the correct picture.

| two |
| nine |
| few |

3. ○○ ○○ _____

4. ○○ _____

5. ○○○ ○○○○ _____

Add **-er** or **-est** to each adjective to complete the sentence.

6. His shirt is _____ than hers. (green)

7. Betsy is the _____ student in the class. (tall)

8. That dog is _____ than the cat. (smart)

It's Time to Take Aim!

On _____ our class will be having a checkup on **adverbs**.
To help your child prepare, please spend about 15 minutes reviewing this skill.

Skill Refresher

Hide the answers at the bottom of the page. Guide your child through the rules and examples below. Then have him complete problems 1–9.

- Some adverbs tell **how.**

safely	gladly
neatly	happily
proudly	sweetly
eagerly	quickly

gently	
slowly	
softly	
loudly	

- Some adverbs tell **when.**

now	today
next	once
early	suddenly

first
soon
never

- Some adverbs tell **where.**

up	under
outside	far

above
everywhere

Target These!

Circle the adverb that tells how.

1. He climbed quickly to the top.
2. Ramone talked shyly to the teacher.
3. The top easily came off the box.

Circle the adverb that tells when.

4. Yesterday we went to the museum.
5. I saw that movie first.
6. Sometimes Ms. Jones sings to us.

Circle the adverb that tells where.

7. She moved the plant here.
8. The dog went inside to get warm.
9. Our house is near the school.

Answers:

1. quickly
2. shyly
3. easily
4. Yesterday
5. first
6. Sometimes
7. here
8. inside
9. near

Checkup 9

Name _____   Date _____

Circle the adverb that tells how.

1. The parrot flew quietly to its perch.

2. Megan sang loudly.

3. The horse ran wildly through the ranch.

Circle the adverb that tells when.

4. He never ate his cake.

5. Today Jess will play chess.

6. We'll go to dinner later.

Circle the adverb that tells where.

7. The snow is everywhere!

8. The vests are inside.

9. The mouse ran upstairs.

Checkup 9

Name _____   Date _____

Circle the adverb that tells how.

1. The lady looked sadly at the spilled milk.

2. Kate placed the doll gently on the floor.

3. The bug crawled carefully over the bench.

Circle the adverb that tells when.

4. I hope the sun shines daily!

5. Earlier she went to the circus.

6. Nate will go first to the store.

Circle the adverb that tells where.

7. His friend moved far from town.

8. The clowns are here.

9. That dollar could be anywhere!

It's Time to Take Aim!

On _____ our class will be having a checkup on **pronouns.** To help your child prepare, please spend about 15 minutes reviewing this skill.

Skill Refresher

Hide the answers at the bottom of the page. Guide your child through the rules and examples below. Then have him complete problems 1–8.

- **Singular** and **plural pronouns** are used to take the place of nouns.

I	me	we	
you	her	they	
he	him	us	
she	it	them	

- **Possessive pronouns** show ownership.

my	mine
his	your
her	its
our	their

Target These!

Circle the correct pronoun to replace each underlined noun.

1. <u>Nicki</u> went to her friend's house. (She, They)
2. <u>Chuck and Ben</u> are playing ball. (He, They)
3. The dog followed <u>Lori and me</u>. (us, them)
4. <u>Toast</u> is best with jelly. (She, It)

Complete each sentence with a pronoun from the box.

her	its	our	mine

5. That CD belongs to me. It is _____.
6. We live in this house. It is _____ house.
7. Sheila bought the cake. The cake belongs to _____.
8. Those papers came from that folder. They are _____ papers.

Answers:

1. She
2. They
3. us
4. It
5. mine
6. our
7. her
8. its

Checkup 10

Name _____ Date _____

Circle the correct pronoun to replace each underlined noun.

1. The zebra has black and white stripes. (You, It)

2. Why isn't Jake coming to the park? (he, they)

3. Kim and I are going to camp. (They, We)

4. Ms. Smith gave the papers to Joe and Linda. (them, her)

Complete each sentence with a pronoun from the box.

| her   your   our   its |

5. These pictures belong to David and me. They are _____ pictures.

6. That is Trish's bike. It is _____ bike.

7. The bird gathered worms. They are _____ worms.

8. The fish belong to you. They are _____ fish.

Test A: Pronouns

©The Education Center, Inc. • *Target Reading & Writing Success* • TEC60874 • Key p. 135

121

Checkup 10

Name _____ Date _____

Circle the correct pronoun to replace each underlined noun.

1. What time will the train arrive? (it, he)

2. Javon and Lou are best friends. (They, He)

3. Karen is on the red team. (It, She)

4. I brought this sandwich for Carl. (them, him)

Complete each sentence with a pronoun from the box.

| my   its   his   their |

5. Bobby has a new skateboard. It is _____ skateboard.

6. That pencil belongs to me. It is _____ pencil.

7. The leaves fell from that tree. They are _____ leaves.

8. Jessica and Jamie have a younger brother. He is _____ brother.

Test B: Pronouns

©The Education Center, Inc. • *Target Reading & Writing Success* • TEC60874 • Key p. 135

It's Time to Take Aim!

On _____ our class will be having a checkup on **subject-verb agreement**. To help your child prepare, please spend about 15 minutes reviewing this skill.

Skill Refresher

Hide the answers at the bottom of the page. Guide your child through the rule and examples below. Then have him complete problems 1–8.

- The subject and verb in a sentence must agree in person and in number.

first person: **I am running** in the first race.

second person: **You are running** in the second race.

third person: **Jan is running** in the third race.

singular: **He runs** twice a week.

plural: **They run** three times a week.

Target These!

Underline the subject in each sentence. Circle the correct verb in ( ).

1. Jill (was, were) going to the store.

2. They (was, were) watching TV.

3. Liz and Sam (is, are) the same age.

4. His snake (is, are) asleep.

5. The tiger (sleep, sleeps) in the sun.

6. I will (bake, bakes) a cake for you.

7. The show (begin, begins) at ten.

8. They (keep, keeps) the door locked.

Answers:

1. Jill (was)
2. They (were)
3. Liz and Sam (are)
4. snake (is)
5. tiger (sleeps)
6. I (bake)
7. show (begins)
8. They (keep)

Checkup 11

Name _____ Date _____

Underline the subject in each sentence.
Circle the correct verb in ( ).

1. Jared (is, are) eight years old.

2. They (is, are) ready for lunch.

3. The ducks (was, were) cold and wet.

4. Kristen (was, were) drawing a tree.

5. Kyle and Johnny (listen, listens) to music.

6. The men (eat, eats) pizza.

7. Nick (like, likes) to tell jokes.

8. The frog (jump, jumps) into the pond.

Test A: Subject-verb agreement

©The Education Center, Inc. • *Target Reading & Writing Success* • TEC60874 • Key p. 135

Checkup 11

Name _____ Date _____

Underline the subject in each sentence.
Circle the correct verb in ( ).

1. Ants (is, are) red or black.

2. Jake (was, were) playing a game.

3. Kent (is, are) rowing the boat.

4. They (was, were) eating apples.

5. Meg (skate, skates) on Saturdays.

6. Russ and Steve (take, takes) turns steering.

7. He (smell, smells) something sweet.

8. They (draw, draws) after math class.

Test B: Subject-verb agreement

©The Education Center, Inc. • *Target Reading & Writing Success* • TEC60874 • Key p. 135

Great aim!

_____
student

is right on target with

_____!
skill

_____
teacher

_____
date

You hit the bull's-eye!

_____
student

hit the mark with

_____!
skill

_____
teacher

_____
date

Answer Keys

Answer Keys

Dog Supplies

Now is the time to buy dog supplies!

Try our new puppy shampoo.

Our doggy beds are soft and warm!

Stock up on Furry Friends dog food.

Your dog will love our tasty treats!

Buy a rubber ball or a chewy bone.

Be sure to pick up a toy too!

Is it time for a new dog-food dish?

We have leashes in all lengths.

Do you need a new dog brush?

We have collars in every color.

Welcome aboard the SS *Hippo!* Captain Potamus will steer the ship. He loves to sail the seas. The captain and his crew take care of the boat. They clean the deck and raise the sail. Captain Potamus also has a noisy pet. Pete the parrot rides on the captain's shoulder. The captain calls out orders to his crew. Then Pete repeats them. Maybe his name should be "Re-Pete"!

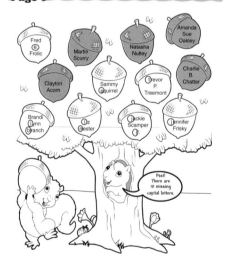

Amanda Sue Oakley

Fred C. Frolic

Martin Scurry

Natasha Nutley

Charlie B. Chatter

Clayton Acorn

Trevor P. Treemont

Sammy Squirrel

Brandi Lynn Branch

Oz Chester

Jackie Scamper

Jennifer Frisky

Psst! There are 10 missing capital letters.

The Mane Town Lions are on the field. Their quarterback, Ron Roar, throws the football. The ball sails past Henry Hall. Next, it flies right through Frank Fur's paws. Just before it hits the ground, Karl King makes an amazing catch! Matt Manesly tries to tackle him. Pete Padfoot tries to bring him down. But Karl gets by them both and scores! Les Lee kicks the extra point. Hooray for teamwork!

Start

March, november, Monday, February, february, Thursday, wednesday, january, April, monday, Sunday, tuesday, June, Friday, april, thursday, Tuesday, May, January, September, August, march, august, october, Saturday, December, may, July

1. Tuesday, January 9 — Tuesday, January 9
2. Sunday, February 12 — Sunday, February 12
3. Friday, March 30 — Friday, March 30
4. Wednesday, April 10 — Wednesday, April 10
5. Saturday, May 22 — Saturday, May 22
6. Monday, June 18 — Monday, June 18
7. Thursday, July 4 — Thursday, July 4
8. Sunday, August 15 — Sunday, August 15
9. Friday, October 26 — Friday, October 26
10. Sunday, December 7 — Sunday, December 7

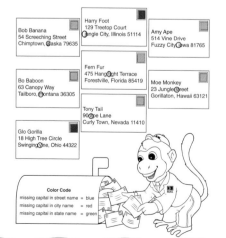

Bob Banana
54 Screeching Street
Chimptown, Alaska 79635

Harry Foot
129 Treetop Court
Jungle City, Illinois 51114

Amy Ape
514 Vine Drive
Fuzzy City, Iowa 81765

Bo Baboon
63 Canopy Way
Tailboro, Montana 36305

Fern Fur
475 Hangright Terrace
Forestville, Florida 85419

Moe Monkey
23 Jungle Street
Gorillaton, Hawaii 63121

Tony Tail
90 Ape Lane
Curly Town, Nevada 11410

Glo Gorilla
18 High Tree Circle
Swingtone, Ohio 44322

Color Code
missing capital in street name = blue
missing capital in city name = red
missing capital in state name = green

Each flower tells the number of errors on the lily pad.

260 Lily Place
Fresh Pond, Michigan

78 Hopping Road
Green Lake, Arkansas

59 Toadstool Avenue
Marshtown, Maine

841 Tadpole Terrace
Newt Swamp, Kansas

577 Ribbit Road
Bubbling Brook, Georgia

143 Big Leap Court
Frogport, Alabama

21 Jumping Street
Streamdale, Illinois

115 Spotted Road
Croakville, Connecticut

1. North America
2. Atlantic Ocean
3. Europe
4. Asia
5. Pacific Ocean
6. South America
7. Africa
8. Indian Ocean
9. Australia
10. Antarctica

1. Bea and Barb Bear hike to Mount Grizzly.
2. Their hike begins at Bat Cave, in the middle of Wild Woods.
3. They row a boat across Snake River.
4. When they reach Sun Valley, Barb takes a picture.
5. At Heart's Hill, the bears stop for lunch.
6. Then they hike through Red Rock Range.
7. They stop to swim in Snow Lake.
8. At the end of Wild Woods, Barb takes another picture.
9. Then they see Mount Grizzly!
10. Next time, they will hike to Mount Flat Top.

"BEAR-RETTES"

Paul Pig loves holidays! The first holiday he celebrates each year is Martin luther king Jr. Day. On Valentine's Day, he gives paper hearts to his farm animal friends. He collects clovers for St. Patrick's day. Each easter, he thanks the chickens for their eggs. He is proud to display the flag on memorial Day, Flag Day, and the Fourth of July! In the fall, Paul dresses up for Halloween. Then he gets ready for Christmas, hanukkah, and kwanzaa. I guess you could say that Paul goes hog-wild for holidays!

Miss Polly Pollen   Queen Bumble
Ms. Y. Jacket   Mrs. Cindy Stripe
Uncle Hank Hornet   Mr. Dave Drone

	Yes	No
1. dr. Frank Finn lives at the north pole.	H	(T)
2. He and Chief Tom Tooth are in a snowman-building contest.	(R)	S
3. One of the judges is mr. Gus Gray.	?	(I)
4. The other judge is queen Wanda White.	C	(B)
5. Last year, Mrs. Sue Sea won the contest.	(E)	V
6. dr. Finn places the head on the snowman.	A	(F)
7. Chief Tooth adds a carrot, some coal, and a scarf.	(S)	L
8. Their friend, ms. Sally Shark, comes to cheer for them.	M	(I)
9. The judge, Mr. Gray, looks at their snowman first.	(O)	W
10. Then he and Queen White give them first prize!	(T)	B

FROSTBITE!

Announcing the
Bug Ball!

There will be a picnic on friday, june 30.
Be sure to join us at
555 ladybug lane
anthill, west Virginia.

On saturday, july 1, we'll have a dance.
Come to
43 jitterbug Avenue
hiveboro, Virginia.

Our picnic rain date is
sunday, august 4.
Don't miss the fun!

LIGHTNING BUGS

the Sea Circus is coming to Wave town! All of the fish want to see it! Mr. and mrs. Shell shark will be there. don dolphin and will whale can't wait to get there. dr. eel wants to see the lionfish. clee Clam loves the clown fish! the swordfish act is a thrill! miss sue starfish puts on a great show! sam seal rides sea horses in the center ring. the cost of each ticket is one sand dollar. it will be a great show!

C   E   S
critter elementary school
presents the

**Best-Ever
Yard Sale!**

M   M
monday, march 22
6:00–9:00

T   T
Find great deals on tim tiger's toys.
B   B
Buy a bike from betty bird.
C   C
Get comic books from carl camel.
S   S
Save on body warmers made by sam snake.
P   P
Taste pam python's freshly squeezed
orange juice.

Join us at
S   R
123 sale road
C   C
critterland, colorado.

If the sentence is complete, add a period in the □.
Color the cherry red.

Remember that a **complete sentence** has a subject and a verb.

Students should have rewritten 2, 4, and 8. Sentences will vary.

	A treasure chest is buried here.	Gold is in the chest.	Jewels might be in the chest.
Many people	The gold	The heavy chest	Use a map to find the chest.
Some people	He has not found the gold.	A man has searched forever.	The chest is well hidden.
Pirate Pete	No one has found the gold.	The key	The pretty jewels
The map	The chest is here.		

1. Does the farmer know Ace is out of the barn ?
2. Where is Ace going ?
3. Ace runs through a field .
4. Ace runs very fast .
5. He wants carrots from the garden .
6. Will the farmer get mad ?
7. Where is the farmer going ?
8. Here he comes now .
9. Is he walking very fast ?
10. The farmer laughs at Ace .
11. How many carrots did Ace get ?
12. Ace and the farmer walk back to the barn .

1. Most kangaroos have large ears**.**
2. Baby kangaroos are called joeys**.**
3. Does the baby live in the mom's pouch**?**
4. Can a kangaroo grow over six feet tall**?**

5. Where do kangaroos live**?**
6. They have tails**.**
7. What do kangaroos eat**?**
8. Most of them eat plants**.**

9. Kangaroos can move fast**.**
10. What is a group of kangaroos called**?**
11. A large group of them is called a mob**.**
12. Are some kangaroos red**?**

Yes	No
U	D
J	E
R	V
H	C
K	H
R	T
B	N
L	A
M	S
T	B
U	X
I	Q

(Circled: U, R, H, K, R, B, T, U, I and E, H, A, S)

IT USES A "HARE" BRUSH!

1. Walt visits the bookstore **.**
2. There are a lot of books on the shelves **.**
3. Where are books about worms **?**
4. Those books are on the top shelf **.**
5. Can Walt reach those books **?**
6. Does the store have books about apples **?**
7. There are five apple books in the store **.**
8. What kind of books about soil are in the store **?**
9. Will Walt buy a book about gardens **?**
10. The garden book is on sale **.**
11. What other books are on sale **?**
12. The store is closing soon **.**
13. What book did Walt buy **?**
14. He bought *Wiggle Workouts for Worms* **.**
15. Walt carries his book home **.**

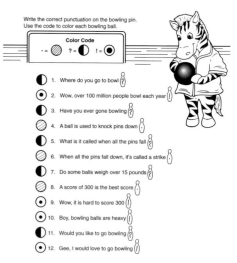

An **exclamation mark** shows strong feeling.

Tom and Tess Turtle like to ski.	They like to ski at Mount Hard Shell.
Look out for the ice.	Wow, there is 30 feet of snow!
Tess went down the slope.	What a steep mountain.
Oh, how the turtles love to ski!	Tom rides the ski lift.
The turtles wear warm clothes!	Tom tries to ski fast.
Hurry up.	Oh no, Tom fell!
Tom and Tess want to rest.	Boy, this was a great day!
Finish	**Finish**

Count the flags to find out who wins the race. **Tom**

Color to show the missing punctuation.

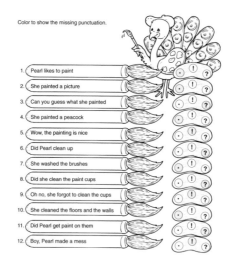

1. Pearl likes to paint
2. She painted a picture
3. Can you guess what she painted
4. She painted a peacock
5. Wow, the painting is nice
6. Did Pearl clean up
7. She washed the brushes
8. Did she clean the paint cups
9. Oh no, she forgot to clean the cups
10. She cleaned the floors and the walls
11. Did Pearl get paint on them
12. Boy, Pearl made a mess

Color Code	
? =	yellow
. =	red
! =	blue

Are all the snakes asleep [?]	Oh no, one snake is still awake [!]	They are under a blanket [.]
Wow, they were up until 11:00 [!]	They watched a good movie [.]	Do snakes snore [?]
What time do snakes go to bed [?]	Oh my, they stayed up late [!]	The three snakes are in one bed [.]
Gee, that one snake snores loudly [!]	They will sleep well tonight [.]	What do snakes dream about [?]

Write the correct punctuation on the bowling pin.
Use the code to color each bowling ball.

Color Code		
. = ⬤	? = ◑	! = ⬤

1. Where do you go to bowl **?**
2. Wow, over 100 million people bowl each year **!**
3. Have you ever gone bowling **?**
4. A ball is used to knock pins down **.**
5. What is it called when all the pins fall **?**
6. When all the pins fall down, it's called a strike **.**
7. Do some balls weigh over 15 pounds **?**
8. A score of 300 is the best score **.**
9. Wow, it is hard to score 300 **!**
10. Boy, bowling balls are heavy **!**
11. Would you like to go bowling **?**
12. Gee, I would love to go bowling **!**

Welcome to the office of Dr. Dragon **.** Oh my, we are sorry you do not feel well **!** Please come in and sit down **.** Where do you hurt **?** How does your throat feel **?** Please stick out your tongue **.** Does your head hurt **?** Let's check to see if you have a fever **.** Do your ears hurt **?** Let's look in your ears **.** Boy, you sure are a good patient, Danny **!** We know you will get well soon **.**

1. January 4**,** 2005
2. March 27**,** 2005
3. April**x** 5, 2005
4. June 10, 2006**x**
5. July 8**,** 2006
6. August**x** 17, 2007
7. September**x** 30, 2007
8. October 12**,** 2008
9. November 1, 2008**x**
10. December**x** 14, 2008

1. March 8, 2005
2. January 31, 2007
3. October 14, 2006
4. July 11, 2007
5. December 20, 2005
6. February 7, 2006
7. May 23, 2005
8. August 2, 2006
9. April 13, 2007
10. November 30, 2005
11. September 17, 2006
12. June 28, 2005

Date

1. January✗ 4, 2005
2. August 20, 2006
3. May 26, 2006✗
4. June 15, 2007
5. July 9, 2005
6. March✗ 3, 2006

Greeting

7. Dear✗ Rover,
8. ✗Dear Spot,
9. Dear Max,
10. Dear✗ Ringo,
11. Dear Sassy,
12. Dear Jack,

Closing

13. Your✗ friend,
14. Best wishes,
15. ✗Love,
16. With love,
17. Yours✗ truly,
18. Sincerely,

Order of answers within categories may vary.

Dates
June 6, 2004
May 3, 2005
July 21, 2006
April 17, 2005
Greetings
Dear Rose,
Dear Ivy,
Dear Daisy,
Dear Poppy,
Closings
Yours truly,
Sincerely,
Love,
With love,

Order of answers may vary.

Denver, Colorado
Salt Lake City, Utah
Juneau, Alaska
Columbia, South Carolina
Montgomery, Alabama
Olympia, Washington
Providence, Rhode Island
Santa Fe, New Mexico
Austin, Texas
Nashville, Tennessee

1. Pete Pig lives in Pink Town, Maine.
2. He drove to Sausage Land, Vermont, to see Pearl Pig.
3. In Pork City, New York, he spent a day at the zoo.
4. He ate soybean salad in Pork Town, Ohio.
5. He stopped in Baconville, Kansas, and bought corn.
6. In Swine City, Colorado, Pete camped in the mountains.
7. Finally, he arrived in Ham City, Utah.
8. Pete and Pearl drove to Pen Village, Oregon.
9. They watched whales in Porkville, Oregon.
10. On his way home, Pete drove through Sty, Texas.
11. Then he spent a night in Chop City, Georgia.
12. He was glad to get home to Pink Town, Maine!

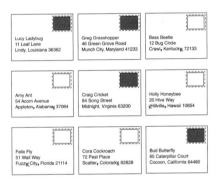

1. Tim, Trudy, and Tom are having a party.
2. They need to plan the food, games, and decorations.
3. Tim will bring hot dogs, chips, and sodas.
4. Trudy will buy a cake, ice cream, and fudge.
5. Tom will bring balloons, streamers, and funny hats.
6. Jen, Jack, and Jill come to the party.
7. The friends play cards, board games, and bingo.
8. Tim, Jen, and Jack sing a song.
9. Trudy, Tom, and Jill clap for their friends.
10. Food, friends, and games make the party a success!

Order of items within sentences may vary.

Moe will buy **shirts, pants, and socks** to wear to school.
At the school supply store, Moe will buy **pencils, paper, and pens**.
Moe shops for **apples, crackers, and cheese** to put in his lunchbox.
He also buys **bagels, chips, and grapes** to eat after school.

Order of items within sentences may vary.

1. Kate likes to paint, bake, and read.
2. Red, green, and blue are the colors she likes best.
3. She can bake muffins, cookies, and cakes.
4. She likes to read mystery, poetry, and joke books.
5. Kate thinks her hobbies are interesting, exciting, and fun.

March 9, 2006
Dear Fran,
How are you? I am fine. I have been keeping busy. During the day, I croak, hop, and watch flies. At night, I sing, play, and clean my lily pad.
I am writing to ask you to go on a trip with me. I will be going to Hopp City, Florida, on May 15, 2006. I would like to stay until May 21, 2006. On the way home, we can stop in Leap Town, Georgia, to visit with Frank. It will be a lot of fun! Please let me know if you want to go with me by May 5, 2006.
I will look forward to hearing from you!
Your friend,
Fred

1. Otto loves to run, jump, and compete in relay races.
2. He trains at the gym in Feather City, Texas.
3. At the gym, he lifts weights, runs laps, and does jumping jacks.
4. Otto set a high jump record on March 16, 2004.
5. He was at a meet in Tall Town, Texas.
6. Otto has also set records in the long jump, the 500-yard dash, and the mile run.
7. His next meet is on June 20, 2004.
8. He will go to Longneck, New Mexico, for the meet.
9. His teammates, Oscar, Ollie, and Opal, will go too.
10. Otto hopes to keep setting records, making friends, and having fun!

1. no
2. yes
3. no
4. no
5. yes
6. no
7. yes
8. no
9. no

ACORN ON THE COB

1. "What's going on?" asked Bess.
2. "A new family just moved in," said Bertie.
3. Bess asked, "Which house?"
4. "The one on the corner," Bertie replied.
5. "I wonder whether they have any children," Bess said.
6. "They don't," Bertie told her. "But they have a cat."
7. "Oh, no!" Bess said, groaning.
8. "Don't worry." Bertie said. "He'll never climb up here."
9. "Are you sure?" Bess asked.
10. "Trust me!" Bertie replied.

1. Shawn whispered to Sheldon**,** "Are you still awake?"
2. "Yes**,**" Sheldon answered. "I can't sleep."
3. "You can try drinking warm milk**,**" Shawn suggested.
4. "I don't like milk," Sheldon replied.
5. Shawn asked**,** "Would you like for me to sing to you?"
6. "No**,**" Sheldon said sadly.
7. Shawn said**,** "You can count sheep."
8. Sheldon shouted, "That's a great idea!"
9. Shawn warned**,** "Just count quietly so that I can sleep!"
10. "I will**,**" Sheldon replied. "Good night!"

1. "Are we there yet [?] " Ork asked [.] .
2. "Yes! Come with me [,] " said Zorf.
3. Sert looked down and asked [,] "What's that green stuff [?] "
4. "That's grass [.] Zorf replied.
5. "Wow [!] "Sert yelled [.] .
6. "Look at all the humans [!] "Ork said, amazed.
7. "Why do they only have two legs [?] "Sert asked [.] .
8. "Well [,] "Zorf said [,] "it's because they only have two shoes."
9. "How strange [!] "Ork exclaimed.
10. Sert smiled and said [,] "We must be smarter than them! "

Accept reasonable responses that are correctly punctuated.

1. "Would you like to dance?" asked Bernie.
2. "I'd love to!" Becky answered.
3. "Wow, you're a great dancer!" Beth said.
4. Burt replied, "Thank you."
5. "I could dance all night!" Bob said.
6. "You're stepping on my feet!" Betty yelled.

1. The team**'s** (jerseys) are red.
2. The skunk**'s** (team) is fast.
3. Each player**'s** (stick) is orange.
4. Each coach**'s** (team) plays hard.
5. The goalie**'s** (gloves) are large.
6. The referee**'s** (whistle) is loud!
7. The rink**'s** (ice) makes skating smoother.
8. The crowd**'s** (cheering) helps the team.
9. Each mascot**'s** (costume) is silly.
10. A game**'s** (ending) can be thrilling.

☑ sharks' swimsuits
◪ cats' bows
⊡ pigs' pants
⊡ rabbits' jewelry
⊠ dogs' hats
⊡ monkeys' shorts
◪ horses' shoes
⊟ gerbils' purses
⊡ snakes' scarves
⊡ birds' shirts

1. two monkey **s'** store
2. a toy **'s** price
3. one skateboard **'s** wheels
4. those puzzle **s'** pieces
5. four doll **s'** clothes
6. a game **'s** board
7. Moe **'s** trains
8. those toy **s'** parts
9. that book **'s** pages
10. a monkey **'s** hat
11. five train **s'** cars
12. a few kid **s'** books

Singular
the gardener's hat
Betty's garden
one dog's collar
a garden's plants

Plural
two birds' beaks
three ladybugs' wings
these buckets' handles
those shovels' handles
those flowers' petals
many plants' leaves

1. they'll
2. I'd
3. don't
4. he'll
5. we're
6. haven't
7. isn't
8. she's
9. I've
10. we'd
11. let's
12. they're
13. it's
14. you've
15. I'm
16. we've

A. we'd, woul
B. should've, ha
C. he'd, woul
D. she'll, wi
E. would've, ha
F. we'll, wi
G. it's, i
H. hasn't, o
I. don't, o

1. I have
2. have not
3. we would
4. they will
5. he is
6. they are
7. does not
8. do not
9. could not
10. you have
11. I am
12. she would
13. it will
14. you will
15. we are
16. can not

Order of answers within categories may vary.

People
Mom
sister
Sam Spider
Wally Webber

Places
bookstore
Spinner City
New York
library

Things
books
spider
July
web

	Person	Place	Thing
1. Welcome to <u>Frogtown</u>!	S	(R)	N
2. This year's jumping contest takes place on <u>Friday</u>.	A	L	(P)
3. The frogs begin on <u>Elm Street</u>.	C	(I)	B
4. <u>Fran</u> cheers from the stands.	(S)	L	E
5. The frogs have been training since <u>May</u>.	O	J	(I)
6. <u>Fern</u> takes the lead!	(E)	H	F
7. <u>Flo</u> is trying to keep up.	(N)	D	G
8. She passes <u>Frank</u> on the corner.	(T)	R	U
9. The race ends on <u>High Street</u>.	V	(M)	C
10. The winner will compete in the finals on <u>Sunday</u>.	B	L	(G)

SPRINGTIME

1. pail, pails
2. shells, shell
3. pails, pail
4. crab, crabs
5. crabs, crab
6. shovel, shovels
7. shells, shell
8. shovels, shovel

Add **-s** or **-es** to make each word plural.
Help Max find the path home.
Color the nine words ending in **-es**.

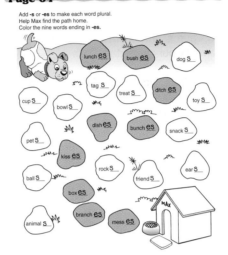

boxes
sandwiches
cities
bushes
parties

skies
wishes
babies
glasses
families

1. glasses
2. sandwiches
3. parties
4. wishes
5. cities

1. Don's coat
2. Amy's helmet
3. Sue's pants
4. Jake's air tank
5. Hal's boots
6. Gus's gloves
7. Hal's boots
8. Sue's pants
9. Jake's air tank
10. Don's coat
11. Gus's gloves
12. Amy's helmet

1. teams' coaches
2. players' uniforms
3. uniforms' colors
4. pitchers' arms
5. players' hats
6. dugouts' benches
7. outfielders' gloves
8. catchers' masks
9. umpires' voices
10. teams' bats

1.	the	green	lake	eat
2.	paper	dog	grab	friend
3.	tree	pack	car	pot
4.	blue	bake	pencil	street
5.	dig	coat	apple	dirt
6.	think	pizza	slow	pretty
7.	wise	save	food	orange
8.	popcorn	soda	run	house
9.	nice	puddle	soft	draw
10.	dark	yes	stir	what

Page 69

Answers will vary.

Playground	Backyard	Kitchen
slide	run	bake
swing	catch	cook
play	mow	stir

Bedroom	Beach	Classroom
sleep	swim	write
read	dig	learn
snore	surf	color

Page 70

The words below should be underlined.
New titles will vary.

1. Soar
2. Laugh
3. Flap
4. Loves
5. Flies
6. Hear
7. Makes
8. Hoot
9. Saves
10. Clean

Page 71

1. I **am** in the kitchen with my mom.
2. Sam, the baby snake, is **hungry**.
3. Sam was not **happy**.
4. Sam and his sister **were** loud.
5. We **were** ready for lunch.
6. The food **is** on the stove.

7. The plates **are** on the table.
8. There was plenty of **food**.
9. We **are** good eaters.
10. The food **was** tasty!
11. Sam and I are **full**.
12. Our **mom** is a good cook.

BY ITS RATTLE!

Page 72

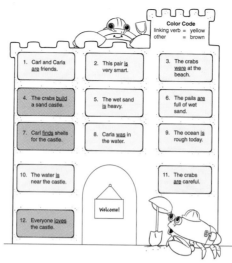

Color Code
linking verb = yellow
other = brown

1. Carl and Carla **are** friends.
2. This pair **is** very smart.
3. The crabs **were** at the beach.
4. The crabs **build** a sand castle.
5. The wet sand **is** heavy.
6. The pails **are** full of wet sand.
7. Carl **finds** shells for the castle.
8. Carla **was** in the water.
9. The ocean **is** rough today.
10. The water **is** near the castle.
11. The crabs **are** careful.
12. Everyone **loves** the castle.

Welcome!

Page 73

The following verbs should be circled.

1. loves
2. wants
3. asked
4. wonders
5. drove
6. paid
7. sits
8. smells
9. buys
10. laughs
11. sat
12. clapped
13. thought
14. wants

POPCORN

Page 74

1. calls, called
2. plants, planted
3. score, scored
4. closes, closed
5. thank, thanked
6. opens, opened
7. chase, chased
8. visits, visited
9. starts, started
10. crashes, crashed
11. search, searched
12. pull, pulled

Page 75

The rocks should be colored for these sentences:

1, 3, 4, 6, 8

9. will put
10. will take
11. will climb
12. will wave

Page 76

Answers will vary.

Color each picture.
Write four adjectives that describe each picture.
Use each adjective only once.

loud	cute	sweet
heavy	slimy	smooth
blue	green	creamy
big	small	yummy

pretty		
yellow		
orange		
tall		

Page 77

1. some
2. two
3. ten

Answers for problems 4–7 will vary.

Page 78

-er	-est
warmer	warmest
faster	fastest
older	oldest
smaller	smallest
longer	longest
darker	darkest

Answers may vary.
1. warmer
2. smallest
3. older
4. fastest
5. longer
6. faster

Page 79

1. newest
2. lowest
3. warmest
4. softer
5. cheaper
6. smaller
7. highest
8. wildest
9. taller
10. cleaner

Page 80

	windy	shorter	helpful
rabbit	monkey	plant	see	crunchy
drink	sunny	smaller	happy	darkest
pencil	furry	phone	grow	paint
days	many	tall	dog	park
walk	house	glad		

Page 81

1. many, playful
2. Two, large
3. three, hungry
4. One, furry, loud
5. five

How many: many, two, three, one, five
What kind: playful, large, hungry, furry, loud

Page 82

Students' sentences will vary.

Page 83

Across
3. Chip's toys are neatly put away.
6. Chip safely gets up on the bed.
8. Chip proudly shows Mom his room.
9. The family eagerly starts the day.
10. Mom gladly packs Chip's lunch.

Down
1. Dad gently shuts the door.
2. Mom quickly fixes eggs.
4. Mom tenderly pats Chip's back.
5. Chip happily dresses for school.
7. Chip sweetly thanks Mom.

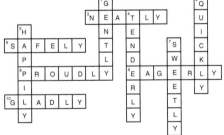

Page 84

1. slowly
2. perfectly
3. softly
4. playfully
5. loudly
6. quickly
7. excitedly
8. wisely
9. easily
10. gladly
11. politely
12. proudly

Page 85

Students' sentences will vary.

Page 86

1. first
2. next
3. before
4. early
5. later
6. suddenly
7. never
8. soon
9. once
10. tonight

iceburgers

Page 87

Circle the adverb on each leaf that tells where.

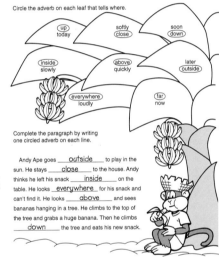

Complete the paragraph by writing one circled adverb on each line.

Andy Ape goes __outside__ to play in the sun. He stays __close__ to the house. Andy thinks he left his snack __inside__ on the table. He looks __everywhere__ for his snack and can't find it. He looks __above__ and sees bananas hanging in a tree. He climbs to the top of the tree and grabs a huge banana. Then he climbs __down__ the tree and eats his new snack.

Page 88

Underline each adverb.
Color each poster by the code.

Color Code
adverbs that tell how = orange
adverbs that tell when = green
adverbs that tell where = yellow

Page 89

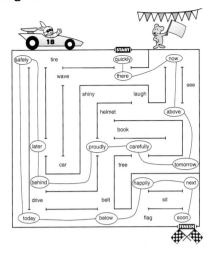

Page 90

1. It
2. us
3. They
4. She
5. He
6. them
7. We

Page 91

1. They
2. He
3. it
4. She
5. him
6. He
7. her
8. It
9. They
10. them

Page 92

1. Sammy
2. Mom, brother
3. apartment
4. brother
5. benches
6. Sammy, brother
7. Mom
8. pen pal
9. Sammy
10. pen pal

1. my
2. his
3. our
4. her
5. your
6. my
7. their
8. her
9. his
10. its

1. (Al) is walking with his friend Ann.
2. The (ants) see something in their path.
3. (Al) claps his hands.
4. (Ann) waves her arms.
5. (Al) and (Ann) squeal, "It is our lucky day!"
6. The ants climb inside the basket and taste its goodies.
7. A lady yells, "Get out of my basket!"
8. (Al) looks at his friend Ann.
9. (Ann) looks at her friend Al.
10. The (ants) run as fast as their little legs will go!

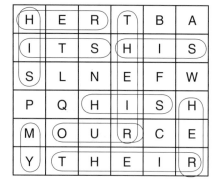

H	E	R	T	B	A
I	T	S	H	I	S
S	L	N	E	F	W
P	Q	H	I	S	H
M	O	U	R	C	E
Y	T	H	E	I	R

1. is
2. is
3. are
4. are
5. is
6. was
7. were
8. was
9. was
10. were

HIS SINGING NEEDS A TUNE-UP!

If the underlined word is correct, put a ✓ by it.
If it is incorrect, put an ✗ on it.
Then write the correct word in the box.

		Dan and Deb love to sail.	They sail each day. ✗ **sail**
Dan sails the boat. ✗ **cleans**	Deb makes lunch. ✓	They go to the lake. ✓	The waves hit the boat. ✗ **hit**
	The sun shines so bright. ✓	The wind blows the sails. ✗ **blows**	
Dan and Deb rest in the sun. ✗ **rest**	Dan reads the paper. ✓	He also steers the boat. ✓	Deb enjoys a good book. ✗ **enjoys**
	She talks on the phone too. ✗ **talks**	They both take a swim. ✓	Dan and Deb ride home. ✓

Find Dan and Deb's course.
Color each box that has a ✓.

1. (Have, Has) you ever been in a hot-air balloon?
2. Some people (like, likes) to race them.
3. Others (drift, drifts) slowly for fun.
4. Balloons (come, comes) in different sizes.
5. Warm air (make, makes) a balloon rise.
6. A large fan (blow, blows) air into the bag.
7. Then a burner (heat, heats) the air.
8. The balloon (rise, rises) slowly.
9. Passengers (ride, rides) in the basket.
10. They (go, goes) up, up, and away!

Students' sentences will vary.

A. driver loves
   fans love
B. crowd waves
   flags wave
C. cars go
   driver goes
D. everyone smiles
   winners smile
E. race takes
   people take

Checkup 1
Test A

1. Lions sleep most of the day.
2. What time do we eat lunch?
3. The books belong to Mr. Cash.
4. Dr. Jones is Rick's doctor too.
5. On Monday, we are going to the park for Veterans Day!
6. School is closed one day in January for Martin Luther King Jr. Day.
7. We will visit the Pacific Ocean this summer!
8. The Grand Canyon has cliffs, a river, and lots of rocks.

Test B

1. How old is your dog?
2. He reads ten pages each night.
3. My dentist's name is Dr. Nelson.
4. The art teacher is Ms. Price.
5. In November we have turkey for Thanksgiving.
6. The Fourth of July is on a Friday this year!
7. There are many types of plants in Asia.
8. The Great Lakes touch several states.

Checkup 2
Test A

1. When do we leave for the circus?
2. Ouch, my shoes are too tight!
3. Keep out!
4. What do brussels sprouts taste like?
5. She would like to buy a football and a soccer ball.
6. I will read my book after dinner.
7. Ben will bring the cake.
8. Who lives in the blue house on the corner?
9. Ellie, be careful!

Test B

1. Wow, it is really dark outside!
2. Oh boy, we're having pizza for lunch!
3. Where is Tony hiding?
4. My favorite book is about a horse and a farm.
5. Texas is in the southern United States.
6. How much longer until we get there?
7. Whom do these belong to?
8. Hey, my friend likes Jell-O gelatin, just like I do!
9. Her birthday is in May.

Page 107

Checkup 3
Test A
1. Man first walked on the moon on July 20, 1969.
2. The new space-age car will be for sale on May 3, 2022.
3. She is from Key West, Florida.
4. Is Atlanta, Georgia, near Macon, Georgia?
5. I want pizza, salad, fruit, and a drink for lunch.
6. After school we can play games, ride bikes, or go to the park.
7. Dear Lee,
   I hope you are having fun at camp. Write soon.
                         Your friend,
                         Nick

Test B
1. Harry S. Truman was born on May 8, 1884.
2. They will buy a new house on August 15, 2007.
3. He lives in Ludlow, Vermont.
4. How far is Salt Lake City, Utah, from here?
5. We brought a tent, a sleeping bag, food, and water on the camping trip.
6. Each night I lay out my clothes, books, and homework for school.
7. Dear Randy,
   Thank you for your letter. I will write you a longer letter soon.
                         Your pal,
                         James

Page 109

Checkup 4
Test A
1. Pam answered, "I'll clean my room right now, Mom."
2. "I love to go sledding in the winter," Blake said.
3. "Jan," whispered Beth, "is that you?"
4. Nia asked, "Is this a new bike?"
5. "No," replied Steve, "I don't have your book."
6. "My favorite fruit is an orange," said Kelly.
7. Roz shouted, "We're going to be late!"
8. "Do you want to borrow my pencil?" asked Les.
9. "First, we went to lunch," Sal said, "and then to the mall."

Test B
1. "It is too cold to go swimming," Shelly said.
2. Lou replied, "I wish I had a dog like yours."
3. "Jill," whispered Ellie, "are you awake?"
4. "Okay," announced Dad, "it's time to go to the dentist."
5. Jeff asked, "Are we going to the game this weekend?"
6. "I eat fish once a week," said Pete.
7. May exclaimed, "Someone gave me a present!"
8. "Do ants like living underground?" wondered Raul.
9. "I liked the first part," Paul said, "but the second part was boring."

Page 111

Checkup 5
Test A
1. one box's top
2. a crab's shell
3. the baby's rattle
4. a few dogs' collars
5. some places' names
6. three computers' screens
7. they've, ha
8. she'll, wi
9. shouldn't, o
10. I'm, a

Test B
1. a bird's nest
2. one writer's pen
3. an orange's seeds
4. two blankets' softness
5. many spiders' legs
6. some books' titles
7. they'll, wi
8. he's, i
9. I'd, woul
10. hasn't, o

Page 113

Checkup 6
Test A
1. Friday, Betty, France
2. cups, tacos
3. glasses, beaches
4. ponies, countries
5. Linda's DVD
6. Ramon's skateboard
7. cars' wheels
8. dogs' collars

Test B
1. Grand Canyon, Helen Keller, Memorial Day
2. zebras, flowers
3. guesses, watches
4. bodies, cherries
5. Donna's headphones
6. Randy's hamburger
7. rabbits' ears
8. buses' seats

Page 115

Checkup 7
Test A
1. listens
2. jumped
3. paints
4. were
5. is
6. past
7. future
8. present

Test B
1. looks
2. wondered
3. roars
4. are
5. was
6. future
7. past
8. present

Page 117

Checkup 8
Test A
1. Red, yellow
2. scared, fearful
3. some
4. couple
5. five
6. younger
7. coolest
8. highest

Test B
1. cold, hard
2. black, huge
3. few
4. two
5. nine
6. greener
7. tallest
8. smarter

Page 119

Checkup 9
Test A
1. quietly
2. well
3. wildly
4. never
5. Today
6. later
7. everywhere
8. inside
9. upstairs

Test B
1. sadly
2. gently
3. carefully
4. daily
5. Earlier
6. first
7. far
8. here
9. anywhere

Page 121

Checkup 10
Test A
1. It
2. he
3. We
4. them
5. our
6. her
7. its
8. your

Test B
1. it
2. They
3. She
4. him
5. his
6. my
7. its
8. their

Page 123

Checkup 11
Test A
1. Jared is
2. They are
3. ducks were
4. Kristen was
5. Kyle and Johnny listen
6. men eat
7. Nick likes
8. frog jumps

Test B
1. Ants are
2. Jake was
3. Kent is
4. They were
5. Meg skates
6. Russ and Steve take
7. He smells
8. They draw

Managing Editor: Sharon Murphy

Editorial Team: Becky S. Andrews, Kimberley Bruck, Karen P. Shelton, Diane Badden, Cayce Guiliano, Njeri Legrand, Deborah G. Swider, Hope H. Taylor, Karen A. Brudnak, Sarah Hamblet, Hope Rodgers, Dorothy C. McKinney, Stacie Stone Davis, Laura Mihalenko

Production Team: Lisa K. Pitts, Pam Crane, Clevell Harris, Rebecca Saunders, Jennifer Tipton Bennett, Chris Curry, Theresa Lewis Goode, Ivy L. Koonce, Clint Moore, Greg D. Rieves, Barry Slate, Donna K. Teal, Tazmen Carlisle, Amy Kirtley-Hill, Kristy Parton, Debbie Shoffner, Cathy Edwards Simrell, Lynette Dickerson, Mark Rainey

©2004 by THE EDUCATION CENTER, INC.
All rights reserved.
ISBN# 1-56234-608-3